THE ARCHITECTURE OF EMPOWERMENT

THE ARCHITECTURE OF EMPOWERMENT
People, Shelter and Livable Cities

Edited by Ismaïl Serageldin

Foreword by Muhammad Yunus

 ACADEMY EDITIONS

Acknowledgements

My thanks go first to Sarwat Hussain, who has been critical in getting this book published. As travelling colleague, assistant and sounding board, he has egged me on to meet deadlines, assisted me in proofing and amending the text, and made sure that despite my responsibilities, my commitments to this project were honoured. His own dedication to the book's subject has been the key to his support.

Likewise, many thanks are due to the Aga Khan Award for Architecture, its Secretary General, Suha Özkan, and its outstanding staff who unstintingly helped me without hesitation at many points in the evolution of the project, especially Jack Kennedy, Farrokh Derakhshani and William O'Reilly.

Muhammad Yunus has been the inspiration for much of this book. His kind words in the foreword reflect the long relationship we have had; though they do not reflect my admiration for what he is doing in the world, the leadership he gives on behalf of the very poor, or my appreciation for what he has contributed to this volume and to the many initiatives we are trying to pursue together.

I am, of course, also most grateful to all the contributors, who have taken time from their busy schedules and have allowed us to use their material. Their commitment to the issues are profound; they represent real practitioners of the architecture of empowerment. Beyond this group of distinguished people are the remarkable achievements of those whose works are the basis of the book's case studies. It is to them, and to the communities concerned, that special thanks are due for having pioneered the best practices that we hope will become the standard practices of all.

Special thanks are also due to other colleagues at the World Bank, especially Mike Cohen, Patricia Annez and Tony Pellegrini, who have done much to shape the message of the Bank on matters of shelter and cities. Mohini Malhotra, Eveling Bermudez and others in the CGAP secretariat have helped me compile the section on micro-finance. My thanks are extended to them and the leading practitioners who make this important enterprise so special. I am also particularly grateful to Dory Morao and the exceptional staff in my office who, above and beyond the call of duty, have helped juggle my messages and correspondence to make the book possible.

Special thanks are due to the many who allowed us to use their photographs and their drawings. They have added much to give the book its liveliness. (Photographic credits are given on page 128.)

Finally, I want to record my deep appreciation to Rachel Bean of Academy Editions, who showed remarkable professionalism and outstanding grace under pressure. She tirelessly worked against very tight deadlines to turn the manuscript into a book. Andrea and Mario Bettella, Alistair Probert and James Powley are the designers who gave the book its present shape. Thanks also to John Stoddart and Maggie Toy who believed in the project and were willing to give it their backing.

With my thanks and appreciation to all, the responsibility for any errors or omissions remains my own.   *Ismaïl Serageldin*

COVER ILLUSTRATION: *From a photograph of East Wahdat Upgrading Programme, Amman, Jordan. (Photo: Hammad Bilal)*

First published in 1997 by
ACADEMY EDITIONS
an imprint of
ACADEMY GROUP LTD
42 Leinster Gardens, London W2 3AN
a member of the VCH Publishing Group

ISBN 1 85490 493 0

Contents

FOREWORD

I have known Ismaïl Serageldin for over ten years, from the time when he asked to visit the operations of the Grameen Bank in Bangladesh, in order to see for himself how the poor can be helped more effectively. His visit was a success. He came away convinced that micro-finance supported the poor and could reach the poorest. He surprised me by reflecting that the most important element of what he had seen in the villages was human dignity, that this lay at the core of a process which was about more than just money. I did not expect that of a high official in international finance; we seemed to be kindred souls.

Subsequently, our paths crossed on many occasions. When the Grameen Bank Housing Programme – featured in this book – was selected for an Aga Khan Award for Architecture, Ismaïl was one of the steering committee. His eloquent defence of the poor, their humanity and their right to a decent exist-ence, and his indefatigable defence of the simplicity of the Grameen designs among the architects, showed me another facet of his commitment and his inter-ests. I was happy that architects who are usually far removed from the interests of the very poor could be engaged so forcefully on the matter of their shelter.

We then joined forces on the Aga Khan Award for Architecture Steering Com-mittee from 1989 to 1992. There I saw his in-depth involvement with architec-tural matters, from theory and criticism to the pragmatic aspects of urban planning as well as finance. Yet he was always concerned with the issue of the large numbers of poor people.

Subsequently, we collaborated on a series of measures to help bring the World Bank closer to the needs of the poor. Despite my early scepticism about the Bank, I found in Ismaïl an important ally in the cause of eradicating hunger and poverty. He was instrumental in involving the World Bank in micro-finance for the poorest, through the creation of the Consultative Group to Assist the Poorest, of which he was elected Chairman. (I joined in chairing the Policy Advisory Group to help this important fledgling effort to fulfil its promise.)

We then worked together on the organising committee of the 1997 Washington Micro-Finance Summit, an important effort, ably organised and supported by Sam Daley-Harris of Results.

In all of this, I have always found Ismaïl a consistent ally in all that I believe in. I was therefore delighted when he informed me that he intended to prepare a book to address architects, and non-architects, on the issues of primary concern to us both. Following in the footsteps of his distinguished compatriot Hassan Fathy, who a generation or more ago called for an 'Architecture for the Poor', Ismaïl Serageldin asked me to support his call for an 'Architecture of Empowerment'. The difference in titles reflects an important shift. It is about challenging architects to do more than build for the poor, or encourage self-help. The architecture of empowerment invites them to rethink the premises of the process of design as much as the process of building. It challenges them to shed their assumed omnipotence and to become enablers for the poor. The idea of empowerment is one that requires commitment, dedication and mental outlook very different to those of conventional architectural practice. I am delighted, therefore, to write the foreword to this book.

If only more in the professions – from architecture, finance, law and so many others – would actually take to heart the idea of empowerment of the poor, we would all be creating a much better world. A world where poverty and hunger are abolished and where the basic dignity of every human being is respected. It is a goal worth striving for. It is attainable. A book such as this, which combines essays by distinguished theorists and practitioners from the fields of architecture and urban planning – such as Ismaïl Serageldin, Suha Özkan, Charles Correa, Arif Hassan, Michael Cohen and Mona Serageldin among others – should serve to enlist the support of many others in these professions. More importantly, it may also help create more contacts and alliances between architects and the social activists who have been at the forefront in the battle against poverty. I am glad that this book is being published to coincide with the Micro-Finance Summit which is also challenging the world to rethink its priorities. I hope that there will be many architects and urban planners who will join others in being the artisans of this architecture of empowerment. We need it urgently.

Muhammad Yunus, Founder and Managing Director of the Grameen Bank

THE ARCHITECTURE OF EMPOWERMENT

A SURVEY

Ismaïl Serageldin

Changing Architecture for a Changing World

Consider the paradox of our times. We live in a world of plenty, of dazzling scientific advances and technological breakthroughs. The Cold War is over, and we are offered the hope of global stability. Yet, our times are marred by conflict, violence, debilitating economic uncertainties and tragic poverty. The cities of our increasingly urban world are witnessing a transformation of their economic base along with intractable unemployment. Civil strife is rampant or threatening. Billions of human beings, especially in the developing world, are living in conditions beneath human decency by any definition.

How is architecture responding to this changing world? Has it adapted its preoccupations and processes to develop a new paradigm as the new millennium dawns? There are, indeed, many distinguished and sensitive architects and urban planners who have joined forces with social activists and imaginative financiers to create what might be called the 'architecture of empowerment'; that is, a built environment which responds to the needs of the poor and destitute, while respecting their humanity and putting them in charge of their own destinies. This book is dedicated to their work.

The architecture of empowerment is not an abandonment of the traditional role of the architect as form-giver, or of the urban planner as land-use specialist; rather, it is an enrichment of these professions. Just as a deeper appreciation of environmental issues does not restrict the creativity of architects, but adds an extra dimension to their work, so this deeper understanding of the needs of the bulk of humanity makes architecture and urban planning – to the extent that they are disciplines concerned with creating a better built environment for humans – more effective and more sensitive professions. Across the multiplicity of disciplines, groups and individuals must come together, it is this improved understanding that will redefine the role of the architect and the planner in relation to the process of change, to the idea of building as process rather than a building as product.

Architects must learn to accord the poor the same respect that they accord their rich corporate clients. Just as they engage in dialogue – often argument –

Conditions below the level of human decency

Hassan Fathy, New Gourna, Egypt – architecture based on local materials and self-help

The house as workplace and home

and listen to the rich corporate clients, so they should with the poor. It is wrong that the poor are always absent from the process (designated by euphemisms such as 'beneficiary' and 'end user'), represented instead by the government agencies that commission architects to work on these projects. The architects and the technocrats presume to know best what the people need, but often the resulting schemes lack any sense of humanity, and fail to provide more than basic shelter and amenities (water, sanitation and electricity). The poor are expected to adjust to the surroundings that are provided. The absence of community links and the lack of concern for the needs of the various community members are all part of the disempowering system that prevails today; a system that the architectural profession has not tried to challenge, but in many cases has only perpetuated. Thus the challenge that faces the design professions is to recognise and deal with the needs of the poor as they would those of the rich.

However, their requirements and priorities are very different. An example of this is the house: for a rich client this may be an individual home, a place designed for residence and relaxation; for a poor client in the Third World it may be far more, a place both of production and shelter. This has been movingly described by Ela Bhatt in her discussion of women's roles in the Third World:

> The home . . . is a productive asset, functioning at various times as a warehouse, a storehouse, and source of inputs such as water and electricity. Access to shelter enables women to work year round, protected from monsoons, floods and other interruptions. The house provides greater security; allows accumulation of material, products, and inventories; and facilitates linkages to services necessary for profitable activities.[1]

It is worth noting in relation to this that the transport systems in the cities of the developing world are designed without regard for the needs of the poorer neighbourhoods and the women in them. They are predominantly focused on the journey to work of those employed in the formal sector, leaving the access roads in poor areas unpaved, unlit and without services. The connections between these neighbourhoods and the rest of the city are left to the vagaries of a very uncertain service provided by entrepreneurial small transport. The problems of

Confused and inadequate transport systems

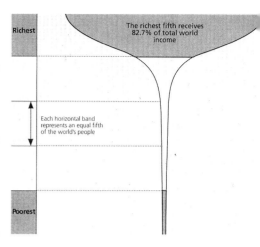

The tremendous inequity in the world is dramatically shown by this 'champagne glass' diagram that indicates that the top 20 per cent of the world's population receive about 83 per cent of the world's income, while the remaining 80 per cent live on only 17 per cent. The poorest 20 per cent live on a meagre 1.4 per cent! This situation is deteriorating. In 1960, the top 20 per cent were thirty times as rich as the bottom 20 per cent, today they are sixty times as rich. (Source: UNDP, Human Development Report, New York, 1992)

Richest

The richest fifth receives 82.7% of total world income

Each horizontal band represents an equal fifth of the world's people

Poorest

security for the women in the poorer neighbourhoods in these circumstances should not be underestimated. The ability of the community to take charge of the physical space between buildings, the public space, not just that of the home, is a central part of the architecture of empowerment.

This open-to-sky space, which architect Charles Correa has so forcefully advocated, is also sorely lacking. Yet, the obstacles to providing it are mostly in the minds of the technocrats who manage public programmes. It is their continued emphasis on housing the poor by cloning a standard unit that is the problem. They do not recognise the dehumanising effect that such spaces have or the need to nest different spaces and scales through the hierarchical progression from public to semi-public to private.

Design for the poor must also leave them options for the future. There should be space for expansion; invariably, the poor build incrementally, and it is necessary to allow for densification. As families grow, they should be able to accommodate the next generation around them, creating stronger links and reducing vulnerability. This helps build the social capital of the community and actually increases their ability to improve their well-being. (Research by Caroline Moser on the coping strategies of four poor urban communities underlines the importance of these extended family links, densification and consolidation of assets in reducing vulnerability.) The case study of the programme in Lima, Peru, shows just how successful such a densification scheme can be.

Is it possible for architects to design in a way that increases the empowerment of people and communities? Or is the creative act of the architect so embedded in the exercise of individuality that it cannot be divorced from the disempowerment of others? After all, the great architects of this century, including Frank Lloyd Wright and Le Corbusier, would never have considered themselves the mere servants of the client. They were, above all, creative artists who were the form-givers of the century. They would not say, as Stanford White had in the nineteenth century, that they would build a client whatever the client wanted. Suha Özkan has traced the evolution of thought among architects primarily concerned with people and communities, those who want to change the world.

Indeed, all great architecture is profoundly human: it invites people to live to the fullest, expresses their desires, and articulates their dreams. It thus requires a somewhat unique mixture of talent, insight and empathy to create such an architecture and to transcend the grand gesture or the capriciousness of the creative individual. For architecture must also be functional, responding to the needs of the clients; that, after all, is what separates it from sculpture.

In the case of the poor, the issue is more complex. The type of architecture that they require is one of empowerment; one that encourages their incremental inputs, that sees building more as process than as product. They must feel that they are the masters of their immediate surroundings, that they have a firm foundation on which to build a better future for themselves and their children. This book demonstrates that this can be achieved, that appropriate conditions of shelter and basic amenities can be attained.

It is published in the wake of the Habitat II world summit held in Istanbul in June 1996, which highlighted the need for dialogue. This conference reminded the world just how much was at stake: that in a generation's time, the urban population of developing countries will treble, and that resultant needs for water and sanitation will stretch the abilities of most governments to respond.

A Changing World

Contradictory Tendencies

The world is subject to contradictory tendencies. Globalisation and homogenisation are at work, while the assertion of specificity – ethnic, religious or cultural – is also present in almost all societies. Globalisation is being driven by the growing interdependence of the world's national economies, and the integration of the financial and telecommunications markets as never before. The political boundaries that divide the sovereign nation-states have become permeable to the ethereal commerce of ideas as well as funds. Globalisation is also driven by the universal drive to respect human rights and to preserve the environment.

Yet, the forces of autonomy assert themselves in practically every society, seeking greater voice and greater power. The positive outcome of this is when communities take charge of their own destinies. The negative side is when autonomy turns to separatism, and specificity to selfishness, which leads to the emergence of hateful petty nationalisms that transform the rightful call for identity and participation into a call for hating your neighbour – and ultimately even 'ethnic cleansing'.

Equally global are the increasing inequities between societies and within societies. Insecurity fuelled by structural unemployment and rising birthrates is the lot of the poor in every society. There is a growing sense of unpredictability about the future. Throughout the rural world, misery and poverty continue as a way of life. Production systems, unchanged for millennia, are being transformed in a couple of generations. No solutions to the global problem of shelter and decent living can ignore the reality of rural poverty and the rapidly transforming economic system to which these populations must adapt – something clearly demonstrated by the highly successful Grameen Bank Housing Programme in rural Bangladesh.

Yet, these problems, though vast, can be dealt with by the people in each village within a broad national or regional framework. The problems of cities are of a different order, for neighbourhoods in cities are not independent villages, they are part of a larger organic whole. They must deal, for example, with the city-wide grid of sanitation and transport, and hence their options and strategies are qualitatively different.

The cities of today, especially in the developing world, are the crucible of all these competing global and local forces. It is in their domain that the challenge is posed most acutely, and it is there that the response is to be found. The world is increasingly an urban place.

An Urban World

Between the first and second Habitat conferences (1976 and 1996) the world population has doubled. The number of cities with populations over five million has grown from about thirty to well over seventy; over sixty are in developing countries. Many of the residents in these cities are poor. If present trends continue, there will be over one hundred million poor people living in cities by 2020.

Rapid urbanisation is a given. Yet, taking place by and large in developing countries, it poses challenges not present in historical urbanisation processes. First, the scale of growth is unprecedented. In India alone, over the next thirty years or so, the increase in urban population will be more than double the total population of France, Germany and the UK combined. Asia's projected urban growth will be equal to nearly half of its current total population. Second, urbanisation will take place with far fewer resources than in the past (when the US was at the same level of urbanisation as Kenya, its per capita income was 50 per cent higher than that of Kenya's today). Third, the communications revolution and the rising expectations of populations everywhere make the increases in inequity particularly visible in the cities and the potential for social pathologies and politically explosive situations more likely. Fourth, as the global economy becomes increasingly interlinked and interdependent, cities face a far more competitive environment as they seek to build their economic and social base.

Convergence and Marginalisation

One of the most interesting features of urbanisation in the 1990s is the common characteristics that can be discerned in cities of both the developed and the developing world. These are vividly discussed by Michael Cohen, who, while show-ing that there are emerging patterns of convergence between North and South, also points out the marginalisation of the South. Aspects of convergence which he addresses include growing unemployment, deteriorating natural environment, declining infrastructure, fiscal crisis, and fraying social cohesion. These conditions, while emanating from different socio-economic dynamics in the developed and developing worlds, nevertheless have similar manifestations. Moreover, they confront mayors and urban managers with a common set of interrelated problems. Whether air pollution, decaying water-supply systems, or grinding fiscal pressures which lead to reduced social services, they all are found in both North and South. It is not surprising that a 1994 United Nations Development Programme (UNDP) survey of 145 mayors from cities in developing countries reported that urban unemployment with its social consequences was their number one problem.

The hypothesis of urban convergence proposed by Michael Cohen is also reflected in popular perceptions such as the visitor from São Paulo who, while in Los Angeles, says: 'I've been here before', or the taxi driver in traffic-choked Bangkok who proudly describing the city traffic says: 'We are modern'. This sense of common predicament provided the basis for consensus at the Habitat II conference where most countries described their urban conditions in terms with which others could identify.

Convergence – or common problems – however, does not imply equal opportunity for remedy. Dar es Salaam has neither the financial nor the technical capacity of Chicago. As a result, it is not surprising that it is less able to contribute to the economic growth of its country or to participate in global patterns of trade and commerce. Thus, whole regions, such as East Africa, find themselves relatively marginalised in the face of competition from more prosperous areas; convergence is already being challenged by growing disparities in income, productivity and opportunity.

These economic patterns have consequences for cultural differences as well, with the homogenising forces of McDonalds, shopping malls and consumer behaviour leading to shared urban experiences. Is this shopping mall in Manila, Munich or Minneapolis? This question is becoming increasingly appropriate in East Asia or Latin America, but as the marginalisation in Dar es Salaam suggests, quite inappropriate in sub-Saharan Africa. This leads to what Saskia Sassen has called the 'new geography of centres and margins'. It is also reflected in culture, with the social distance between traditional cultures, and their ability to communicate with one another, affected by growing economic disparities. The resulting ethnic differences are also reflected in social tension and conflicts.

Examples from the North

The cities of the North that Michael Cohen talks about are able to draw upon many more resources than the cities of the South. But there are poor people in rich countries just as there are rich people in poor countries. Reaching the poorest in the North is difficult but not impossible. The most successful schemes seem to have been related to empowerment, community involvement and micro-finance. Not surprisingly, there are similarities between such schemes in both the South and the North. This is exemplified by the Shore Bank scheme in Chicago and the Grameen Bank programme in Bangladesh.

In 1973, Shore Bank Corporation – a development bank holding company in the business of increasing opportunities in under-invested communities – bought South Shore Bank to develop a unique, cost-effective housing-rehabilitation strategy for rundown Chicago neighbourhoods. Since then, the bank and its affiliates have financed the rehabilitation of about 30 per cent of the twenty-five thousand

Crowded streets in an Indian city   *The impressive skyline of New York*

apartments in South Shore, a Chicago suburb, helping rescue an economically depressed black neighbourhood. Operations have been consistently profitable, and Shore Bank's loan-loss figures compare favourably with those of similar-sized banks. Last year's losses were 0.675 per cent of loans outstanding.

Shore Bank relies on the Grameen Bank model which uses peer pressure to assure repayment of small loans. Shore Bank's success has demonstrated the importance of investing in people and their productive capacities; of the role of banks in convincing other financial institutions to invest in underprivileged communities; of scale; and of combining the power of the private sector's investment methods with the social goals of the public sector. A key ingredient in its success has been the ability to attract deposits from outside the bank's home market, reversing the normal pattern of banks collecting deposits in poor communities and making loans in other areas.

Shore Bank's operations have been so successful in empowering communities that the model is being replicated in Arkansas, Kansas and Michigan. Such attempts will need to be nurtured so that the process of empowering underprivileged communities can occur at a larger scale.

The Special Case of Developing Countries

Cities of the South suffer particular problems caused by the rapid pace of urbanisation and change. Population growth, influx of rural migrants, and an evolving economic base, all challenge the ability of the cities to provide jobs and livelihoods. Crumbling infrastructure, poor and over-stretched social services, rampant real estate speculation, and weak governments all contribute to put tremendous pressure on cities, which are often loci of invaluable architectural heritage; while the degradation of the urban environment limits the abilities of a growing, shifting homeless population to take root and establish communities with a minimum standard of decent housing. The animosities between groups and tensions within the cities fray the social fabric as much as economic speculation transforms the urban tissue. The historic city centres are increasingly ghettoised, as the middle class and economic activities either flee or actively destroy their very fabric.

Restoration and adaptive reuse, old
Sana'a, Yemen

Bukhara, Uzbekistan – restoration of the old
city core and its integration with the new

Case Studies of Success

Against this spiral of mounting problems, a profound change in the way we do
business is required. It is possible to mount a concerted challenge, one that will
install a vigorous positive spiral of rising incomes, improved services, and increased
social solidarity. The nineteen case studies presented here, all internationally
recognised success stories, demonstrate the various facets of the successful response.
They show that all of the measures advocated can indeed work, and that they
hold out the promise of more success. For we have yet to see the full power of
these models; the time is still to come when they are combined in the same city,
to realise the full synergies of which they are capable, bringing about the positive
spiral that we are advocating. The case studies are grouped according to some
of the concepts that are central to a comprehensive response to existing conditions.

Redeeming the Legacy of the Past

Every culture defines itself at least in part by what it cherishes of its past heritage.
The built environment is an important if not essential part of that legacy, though
in many cities of the developing world it is being destroyed. Successful responses
to this share certain characteristics. They stress the integration of the historic
core into the overall fabric of the city, recognising its special attributes and
contributions. They also focus on the adaptive reuse of individual landmark
buildings and protect the special urban character of the area, something that
requires attention to street alignment, scale, volumetric aspects of new construction,
and the mix of land uses. This book contains case studies of success in mobilising
local talent and creativity to conserve the legacy of the past, but as part of a
living, thriving, growing city.

Sana'a, Yemen, is a telling example of the co-ordination of all the stake holders'
efforts within an overall framework. Here, individual houses were restored and
reused. Roads were paved and the entire sanitation system was upgraded to
help protect the old historic core from further degradation. The lesson here is
that piecemeal actions can be positive, if they are guided by a general overview.
This overview and guidance, however, must come from the residents themselves.

Lamu, Kenya – a unique project to conserve and adapt the heritage of East Africa   *Hafsia Quarter, Tunis, Tunisia – a rare example of a successfully revitalised city centre*

The restoration work in Bukhara, Uzbekistan, has a different background. Here, residents were involved in a campaign to save some of their most important monuments, but the loss of central government support following the break-up of the USSR meant that they had to continue the restoration work from their own resources. The integration of the old city into the fabric of the whole is now complete, and the restored core has generated substantial new economic activity around it. Some old *madrasas* have been reused as community centres while others have retained their vocations as educational establishments.

Lamu, in Kenya, presents yet another case. The conservation of the old town with its magnificent housing is a landmark effort that marks the first comprehensive conservation plan developed and enacted with the involvement of the local community in East Africa. The programme is important because it incorporated a detailed study of the social fabric and the economic structure of the historic town, as well as its architectural characteristics. It went beyond establishing a comprehensive conservation plan and design guidelines, and focused on the active involvement of the local community in priority setting and providing training programmes for the restoration and maintenance of the building stock. The reality of the enterprise was also tested in demonstration projects focusing on the rehabilitation and improvement of public spaces and buildings.

To the extent that the preservation of the legacy of the past is part of creating an enabling and empowering environment that helps people establish their sense of identity, the efforts described above are all part of creating more livable cities. They provide their residents with the pride of self-knowledge and the motivation to identify with community and place.

Revitalising the City Centre
The central areas of many cities in the developing world pose special challenges. Some contain historic cores that have become run-down and ghettoised, the dwelling place of poor migrants. Others, though capable of providing the formal sector with the spaces necessary for its commercial activities, are unable to cope with the needs of the poor, who are then pushed to set up illegal hawker stands

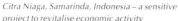

Citra Niaga, Samarinda, Indonesia – a sensitive project to revitalise economic activity

Asilah, Morocco – the impetus for economic revitalisation came from a cultural revival

and street vending operations, always at the mercy of the next police raid. Entire cities, usually small and of special character, are also finding that they are unable to maintain an economic base vibrant enough to deal with the needs of a new generation of job seekers.

Nowhere is this more true than in the historic city centres in the Muslim world, the medinas. These treasures of architectural and urban heritage are victims of crumbling infrastructure and real-estate speculation. They have deteriorated into dense and insanitary areas, becoming home to the poor. Here the inner districts are increasingly suffering from the economic sclerosis created when the middle class and new economic activities leave to go elsewhere.

Against this background, the Hafsia Quarter in Tunis, Tunisia, represents an exemplary success in revitalising the economic base and diversifying the social mix of the inhabitants of the old medina. The middle class has returned, restoring it as the locus of social and economic integration. This is a unique success in reversing the negative trends seen in so many cities of the Muslim world.

Citra Niaga in Indonesia shows that a participatory approach is suitable to handle the problems associated with the creation of an integrated commercial development in which street hawkers are given a legal space in which to ply their trade and a voice in the design of that space. By so building on the existing informal economic activities of the neighbourhood, this development was both a commercial and an architectural success.

The city of Asilah in Morocco was facing a decline in its economic base and a degradation of its building stock; it needed a major effort to reverse this. Under the leadership of some of the more important citizens, a number of key residences were restored or renovated, the community then pitched in to repave the streets and repaint the walls, and a cultural festival was organised. The result was a dramatic success and the Asilah summer festival became a major event in the cultural life of the country, attracting many visitors and renowned artists from Morocco and abroad. The city's economy has been given a big boost and the renovation efforts have given the city a new sense of pride, all based on the voluntary efforts of the local community.

Lublin, Poland – the community revitalised its shops while upgrading the housing

In the Polish city of Lublin the local community was instrumental in maintaining the old city fabric and generating many new businesses during the process of regularising and upgrading the housing of the area. Their example was praised at the Habitat II conference.

Reaching the Poorest: The Rural World

The view that the most poverty-stricken in the rural world can neither be reached nor afford decent, albeit modest, housing has been effectively refuted by the Grameen Bank's in Bangladesh. The Grameen Bank, which empowers the poor through micro-finance, has had notable success in fighting poverty. It serves the needs of some of the most impoverished people in the world: the landless rural women of Bangladesh, who constitute the vast bulk of the bank's 1.5 million borrowers and who are also its owners. The Grameen Bank lends US$20 million each month and is working in 32 thousand villages in Bangladesh. It provides loans averaging US$100 and enjoys a repayment rate averaging 98 per cent, far better than most 'development banks' lending to entrepreneurs in developing countries.

The ability of the Grameen Bank to reach its membership and mobilise savings for housing has been demonstrated spectacularly. The Grameen housing programme was based on making available a minimal structure, roofing material and sanitary facilities that could be built by the people themselves, with a reliance on local materials and self-help techniques. The whole costs US$300 which is repaid over ten years. The Grameen Bank was able to extend loans to 45 thousand people in less than three years, and today reaches over 340 thousand. The results were so successful that the programme received the Aga Khan Award for Architecture in 1989.

Reaching the Poorest: The Urban World

Against a background of inadequate government response to the housing needs of the poor in Pakistan, the institutional challenges are explored by Arif Hassan in an attempt to lay the groundwork for effective action (action probably best exemplified by the Orangi Pilot Project in Karachi).

Grameen Bank Housing Programme, Bangladesh – enabled the rural poor to have their own homes   *Orangi pilot project, Karachi – famous for its provision of sanitation systems and housing*   *Khuda-Ki-Basti, Hyderabad – provided incremental housing and a sense of community*

This major effort succeeded in reaching six hundred thousand poor with housing and services; it did so at about one tenth of the official prices estimated by the Karachi Development Authority had it proceeded in its conventional manner.

The challenge of the Orangi scheme was to put local people in charge. The sequence of their priorities was the opposite of that which engineers tend to assume. First they wanted access to water and a working sanitary facility in the home, then they wanted to remove the waste from the home, and then from the neighbourhood, and only then worry about connecting it to the main trunk connections to the treatment plant. This reverse sequence was exactly how the project was implemented by the people themselves. The public authorities contributed only to the trunk connection and the treatment plant. When it came to housing, the same principles were applied. The programme worked with existing informal institutions, known as *thallas* (building material warehouses-cum-contractors), and the local people to bring about impressive results.

The Khuda-Ki-Basti Incremental Development Scheme in Hyderabad, Pakistan, shows that it is possible to reach the homeless and give them the opportunity to create a community of their own. Homelessness accompanying extreme urban poverty is on the rise everywhere: it is going to be a major challenge in the cities of the developing world. In Hyderabad, the key is access to land that does not get hijacked by the middle classes. The project is based on a sensitive participatory process which identifies the truly poor and homeless through a screening process that involves a two-week waiting period in a reception site. It gives the participants a sense of dignity by access to ownership. It involves them, through payments, in the selection of the improvements that will be provided.

The actual housing is built incrementally as their incomes allow, and the social transformation is profound and inspiring. An NGO, created by the initiators of the project, is now working with the community to improve the building and the architecture of the housing. This project, which has successfully reached those who remain unreached in so many societies, is financially sustainable and economically viable, and deserves widespread recognition and replication.

Kampung Improvement Programme, Jakarta – a transformation of one of the poorest slums

East Wahdat, Amman – a poor slum transformed into a thriving community

Upgrading the Slums and Densification

The provision of adequate water and sanitation services for the poor does not need to be expensive to the public treasury. In fact, the choice of technology in relation to density can make a dramatic difference in the cost per person served. However, it is evident that the enormous numbers of people that need to be served – numbers which will increase over the coming generation – pose a challenge of a different nature. It is the way that the policies governing these sectors and projects are designed and implemented that must be changed. The success stories involving large numbers almost invariably depend on the mobilisation of the people concerned to take charge of their future, with the support of others.

Thus, the Kampung Improvement Programme (KIP) in Jakarta – arguably the largest effort of its kind – has been an enormous success, largely because it changed the policy framework and provided incentives for people to take charge of millions of tiny improvements. The state focused on supplying secure tenure and paving the streets. Provision of water supplies came later. The minimum levels of service adopted initially made it possible to provide very large numbers of people with open drains and later on with covered networks. The KIP in Jakarta received one of the first Aga Khan Awards for Architecture, and subsequent KIP programmes in Surabaya and Yogyakarta were also honoured (though the latter added new dimensions of self-expression for the communities concerned, going way beyond the provision of the basics exclusively focused on by the initial projects).

The case of the East Wahdat Upgrading Programme in Amman, Jordan, is equally impressive. It is marked by a total transformation of the physical appearance of the built environment, where a fetid slum has become a thriving middle-class suburb in the course of a decade. The industry of the residents and their access to the credit necessary to upgrade their dwellings, supported by a secure tenure and the confidence of an administration that believed in them, combined to bring about nothing short of a total transformation of the neighbourhood. Titling, credit, technical assistance and links to the basic infrastructures were all that was needed to make the miracle happen. This particular World Bank-financed project won an Aga Khan Award for Architecture in 1992.

Lima, Peru – densification of the urban fabric allows the poor to change their own environment

Shushtar New Town, Iran – a sensitive scheme using traditional materials and techniques

Ismailia, Egypt – empowered thousands of families to create their own habitat

Lima, Peru, was the site of an important project for community building. Urban planner Gustavo Riofrío of DESCO, a Peruvian NGO, organised a programme here to deal with densification and its consequences through community participation supported by sound technical inputs. Without such technical assistance, additions often pose a risk to the safety of the inhabitants. Nevertheless, a sensitivity to local concerns remained at the core of the programme, and residents set the agenda and extensions of credit to match the programme implementation needs.

Building New Settlements

The architecture of empowerment doesn't consist solely of improving existing urban conditions, it also plays a vital part in the creation of new settlements. In this important area we present two case studies of successful schemes. Shushtar is a new town in Iran designed to house workers from an industrial plant nearby. The overall scheme, handled with great sensitivity by the architect Kamran Diba, creates humane, inviting spaces with a minimum of expense. Using the same simple construction materials – brick, reinforced concrete and plaster – the architect has been able to create an inviting human-scale community, which recaptures and reinterprets the tonalities of local architecture and the rhythm of its rooftops, and allows the families to find their own havens of privacy. The quality of brickwork and the attention to detail shows that great elegance can be achieved without excessive cost. The city as a whole functions well and has received international recognition.

The Ismailia Development Project in Egypt has been a dramatic success in mobilising local residents to create an entire community with the assistance of the government in dealing with issues of titling, access to credit, and linking up with the basic infrastructure. The emergence of the corner stores and the busy community activity speak for the bonds that go beyond the mere proximity of people to the sense of solidarity that defines community in an emerging new development.

*Aranya, India – sensitive design and a building
process that encouraged community feeling*

*Yogyakarta, Indonesia – one of the poorest,
most marginalised of slums was transformed*

Creating Communities

It will already have become obvious that an important part of empowering people comes through the creation of social bonds and a sense of community. The Aranya Low-Cost Housing Project in Indore, India, is a major contribution to addressing the problems of housing the poor and improving social harmony at a time of tension and rising social strife. The architect, Balkrishna Doshi, replaced the insensitive grid so frequently associated with sites-and-services projects with a more suitable urban design layout. It attempted to provide an architectural vocabulary suitable to the socio-economic circumstances and the climate, and showed in the first eighty architect-designed units how this could be achieved. By providing the vocabulary and a small utility core, the opportunities were provided to build repeatable and affordable units. These units, while obeying a series of standardised requirements for utilities and foundations, could be permutated endlessly into a rich and provocative statement about low-cost housing. The original architect-built model was able to promote and sustain variations that were produced indigenously in the spirit of the community, their diversity adding to the spirit and variety of the original intention.

However, even more important than the design goals of the project are the social goals that it promotes. By creating common spaces, arranging for the shared completion of neighbourhood facilities, and mixing Muslims, Hindus, Jains and others in these neighbourhoods, the project promoted co-operation and neighbourliness and the tolerance of diversity. It seems to be succeeding in the provision of conditions to promote the desired cohesive social relationships. In addition, it is actively providing a socio-economic mix that allows for cross-subsidies and financial viability. This is an unusually sophisticated scheme that should be widely studied: in a world of intolerance and strife, it is a beacon for what enlightened and socially responsible architecture can achieve.

The case of the Yogyakarta Kampung Improvement Programme in Indonesia is different in that it is a small community that literally created an identity, a sense of self, in addition to being able to upgrade and improve the conditions of the poor. It was very much about organisation, empowerment and a sense of pride.

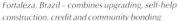

Fortaleza, Brazil – combines upgrading, self-help construction, credit and community bonding

Curitiba, Brazil – sound environmental management and progressive transport policies

The Fortaleza Community-Based Urbanisation and Favelas Rehabilitation Programme, Brazil, was selected out of some six hundred submissions as one of the twelve best practices at Habitat II. It is designed around strengthening community bonds, and has several interlinked objectives: to upgrade, to promote self-help construction supported by credit, and to reinforce community bonds. It differs from conventional sites-and-services projects by ensuring that resident participation is at the core of every programme activity; by selecting project locations to maximise spillover effects and shape urban growth; by making job creation an essential objective; and by relying on people being stake holders not 'beneficiaries'. This has meant community control of the development process. The programme relies on providing credit to the poor. Governance ensures that all the stake holders are represented: the community, the NGOs, the state and municipal governments, the university and the technical school.

Managing the Urban Environment
The case of Curitiba is important. The long stream of its environmental management successes has been widely discussed, particularly its ability to reduce automobile traffic and to involve its citizens in widespread recycling of waste. Environmental successes, however, require more than administration and sound technical solutions. They are about changing people's behaviour. They are about empowerment. In Curitiba there is a continuing process of empowerment through stake-holder involvement which gives individuals and communities confidence in their ability to manage the city. Over the last thirty years this has been matched by a stream of innovations from an engaged population. The establishment of an 'Open University for the Environment' has resulted in a widely informed population, from all income levels and social origins. This has led to a shared sense of civic and environmental responsibility.

These case studies show that a concerted response to all the aspects of the problem of rapid urban growth – poverty, environmental degradation and the empowerment of the poor – is not only possible, but tends to create synergies that reverse the negative spiral of paralysis and decay. The keys are empowering the poor and promoting a sense of community by involving all the participants, and getting their roles right in addition to getting the costs rights.

Distilling the Lessons

A successful response to the issues of poverty, shelter and cities requires consensus between diverse interest groups if sustained progress is to be made. Participation is the key to achieving this. But to be meaningful, participation must be about real decision-making not peripheral issues.

Change must be addressed and assimilated in such a way that the citizens of each city will be able to craft their own future. This does not mean that architects have no role. Indeed, they are the skilled individuals who can help define a sense of place by giving it its landmarks, just as urban planners can help craft the enabling environment that will protect the legacy of the past while allowing room for the future. They must both work to ensure that the poor become the artisans of their own destinies.

The mayors and city and local governments understand the urban challenges and know the human cost of failing to rise to them. They are also increasingly aware of the limits of their public resources and the need to harness the private sector's investments and the involvement of local communities, without which quality of life issues cannot be addressed. All concerned parties must actively get involved in rethinking government, how it is structured, and, most importantly, how it serves its citizens, especially the poor and the weak.

External aid programmes should actively support this building of new relationships. Donor-financed programmes should be based on inclusive processes as they are critical to the creation of successful communities. However, participation should not just be about reserving some funds in project preparation for a few well-connected NGOs; it should be about helping local and central governments to establish relationships with the whole range of formal and informal groups that articulate the needs of various sections of the community, mobilising them to make cities work better. The action agenda must be organically linked to a process of forging alliances between the international community, national and local governments, and neighbourhood groups and NGOs to ensure that lofty ideas are followed up with action on the ground.

Lessons Learned

The key lesson is that solutions lie in the cities themselves. The innate genius of the local people must be harnessed and their potential unleashed to bring about lasting, profound and sustainable solutions to the problems of cities in the developing world. The question is how? It will require a substantial change in the way people do business and the manner in which government is organised. Above all, it will involve empowering the poor to make the difference and to take charge of their own destinies. On the public sector side this requires several things.

Louis I Khan, National Assembly Building,
Dhaka, Bangladesh – a landmark building

Public Sector: Rethinking Government

Rethinking Government has many dimensions. National governments, the external financier's traditional partners, have become too distant to handle the needs of their citizens as individuals, and hence they must devolve such responsibilities to local governments.

It should be emphasised, however, that in advocating these ideas we are not supporting the maxim that he who governs best governs least; nor are we replacing the failed ideology of statism with an almost mystical belief in markets and the private sector. What is needed is good effective government. The ruthless efficiency of the market as an allocating mechanism must be tempered by a nurturing and caring state. Indeed, the market itself needs an efficient and effective state in order to work: law, contracts, courts and property rights are all essential.

So what are the changes required? They concern the levels and functions of governments, the creation of genuine public/private partnerships, and the recognition of the role of the community as well as the individual in forging the new urban reality. Yet, none of these changes will successfully materialise if we do not change the rules of finance, accountability and incentives.

Public Sector: Institutional Change

Experience has shown that cities have not been served well by the highly centralised decision-making that has often dominated urban management. Cities may have had nominal responsibility for a wide range of functions, but many local governments were, in practice, excluded from decisions critical to the quality of urban life. Virtually all investment decisions – from sanitation to storm drains, from slum upgrading to rehabilitating local schools – were at the initiative of central governments or external financiers. Local governments were left to maintain investments they didn't choose, and to mobilise revenues on a very narrow and distorted tax base.

The problem with this system in so many instances was more subtle than the obvious and very real problem of identifying local needs from a central vantage point. The more subtle and insidious problem was accountability, and decentralisation will not automatically solve this problem. Fundamental reform of local service delivery must be based on unambiguous, transparent and realistic assignments of responsibility so that the individual citizen knows 'where the buck stops' if their garbage is not collected or their neighbourhood does not get reliable water supplies.

If government is to be genuinely accountable, the financing of cities and towns needs to change. Typically, the system of financing key local services is riddled with perverse incentives. Local tax bases and user charges are highly political and often tightly controlled by central government. As a result, they have been marginal to city financing. Central revenues are an alternative but are unpredictable and distributed in a highly arbitrary manner. So, what needs to be done?

— In many cases, it will be necessary to devolve power over certain taxes and user charges. For example, should local water utilities have to provide water subsidies determined nationally when they reach only a small, privileged group of users and local government wants to expand service to the poor? Or when their local government has decided that demand for water needs to be managed far more aggressively if long-term needs for all are to be met?

— In many cases, local governments should be paid for providing services to the poor because they can be effective as the agent of central government in executing national programmes. Primary education is an example: it is one of the most important in-kind transfers to the poor, has benefits at the national level, and should not be funded only on the basis of local choices. At the same time, local governments can sometimes manage the system more in accordance with local preferences than the centre. A good transfer system can make this division of labour effective.

— Central transfers should be based on criteria that include managerial and financial performance as well as local need. Such transfers should reward cities that have maintained past investments, are able to cover the recurrent costs of operating their facilities, and are transparent, responsive and inclusive in investment decisions.

— Central governments need to manage the macro-economy soundly so the financial system can develop in a way that provides access to well-managed local governments.

— If devolution is to work for cities a new relationship must be forged between local governments and their constituents – between the slum dweller, the urban unemployed, the captains of industry, the growing middle class, and the emerging civil society. As Jaime Ravinet, Mayor of Santiago, has said: 'The only way to develop a city to a human scale is to have the participation of the people.'

Making that relationship work is far more complex than having or not having local elections. But new practices are emerging that point in positive directions. More cities need to follow the lead of Bangalore which has initiated a report card on the quality and responsiveness of government services or of Seoul which operates citizen complaint reporting centres and holds regular days of dialogue with the citizen.

Inadequate systems of water supply, Jakarta, Indonesia

Within cities, neighbourhoods like Orangi in Pakistan should be the first in line for access to trunk infrastructure. Local governments need to be more entrepreneurial in seeking out private sector partnerships, like the AGETIPS in Africa, to focus on short-circuiting heavy government processes for activities like works contracting and supervision, and to help build the credibility essential to mobilise citizens to pay for and 'own' local services. More mayors need to build political consensus around improving basic services, as did the Mayor of Tijuana (Mexico) who successfully forged a coalition for flood control investments funded out of a local betterment levy.

Private Sector

Much of what has been said of the public sector also applies to the private sector. However, the private sector requires an enabling environment to function, and this cannot be seen in isolation from the issues of governance. Transparency, accountability, institutional pluralism, the rule of law and participation are the key features of good governance, without which no development programmes are likely to be effective.

The incorporation of the private sector is essential in any long-term solution to the creation of livable cities. It is the engine of growth, and growth is an essential ingredient in any effective fight against poverty. The provision of a viable economic base in cities will depend on the private sector, but two qualifiers are needed. First, the private sector does not mean just giant transnational corporations, or even the large-scale national private sector, it also means the thousands of tiny enterprises in the informal sector and the micro-enterprises that provide millions of people with livelihoods. Second, the private sector does not mean the perpetuation of ugliness, or of one-sided exploitation as shown in the creation of the new marketplace at Citra Niaga in Indonesia.

The Civil Society

Within that context, the role of the civil society is essential. NGOs and CBOs as an important part of civil society are now becoming full partners in the design and implementation of development programmes and projects. Increasingly, as the nation-state has to redefine its role to become enabler and regulator, and as the private sector takes on the role of engine of growth, so the civil society – especially women's groups – becomes the essential force to hold communities together and to reach those members of society that are not easily reached by the formal institutions of the modern state.

The Role of International Development Assistance

The future of cities in developing countries will primarily be determined by the people of those countries. Their determination, their commitment, and their vision must address issues of poverty and basic well-being to ensure that every person has the minimum that so many of us take for granted.

Yet, international development assistance does have a role to play, to provide a helping hand, to give well-targeted and judicious investment that will accelerate the process and help those who help themselves. The manner in which this assistance is provided is essential to its effectiveness. It must be based on a real sense of partnership, not on a donor/recipient mentality. Experience shows that only those programmes that are truly 'owned' by the developing countries have a chance of sustained success. Such programmes must therefore be 'nurtured' through dialogue, mutual respect and understanding. Development programmes cannot be forced. They cannot be imposed from the outside, no matter how noble the motivations. Development is like a tree, it can be nurtured in its growth only by feeding its roots, not by pulling its branches. It is therefore important to support programmes that encourage private initiative, the empowerment of the weak and the marginalised, and the promotion of a vibrant civil society, all of which are key ingredients in promoting sustainable development. In this context, constructive multi-party dialogue is important, dialogue that should engage governments, both national and local; civil society, both national and international; the private sector; and the World Bank and other international financiers.

Empowering the Poor

If the poor are to improve their own well-being, generating their own improvements rather than receiving charity, several areas have to be addressed: the provision of assets to the assetless, the provision of basic services, and the provision of credit through micro-finance. This last point is so important that a special section of the book has been devoted to it.

The success of pioneers like Muhammad Yunus of the Grameen Bank has encouraged the growth of a world-wide movement in support of the idea of micro-finance: providing the poorest with access to micro-loans that enable them to raise themselves from poverty. The record is so impressive that in 1995 the World Bank and a group of the most important financing agencies formed the Consultative Group to Assist the Poorest (CGAP) to promote the provision of the best practices in the micro-finance field. Micro-finance involves two types of lending: to micro-enterprises (for tiny enterprises that employ usually less than five people and are frequently, if not invariably, in the informal sector), and to individuals, through solidarity groups, for self-employment among the poorest.

The track record of well-run micro-finance institutions is impressive. Most of the borrowers are very poor women. The repayment rates are invariably over 95 per cent, and the impact of access to such credit results in dramatic improvements in the conditions of life for the poorest. In one study of the Grameen Bank it was found that the women who borrowed successive loans over an eight year period had a 48 per cent chance of pulling themselves and their families above the poverty line. The corresponding figure for villages not served by Grameen was about 4 per cent. Thus, access to micro-credit along with the other features of the programme, including savings and solidarity groups, increase their chance by a factor of twelve. Furthermore, such women have double the contraception acceptance rate leading to fewer infant deaths, and better nourished and educated children. A remarkable achievement.

It is the success of projects like this that have led to the Summit on Micro-Finance in Washington in 1997, the purpose of which is to convince the world to engage in a campaign to reach one hundred million borrowers among the poorest in ten years. The effort is world-wide and is aimed at the industrialised countries as well as the poorest developing countries.

The provision of decent shelter and the design of livable cities is almost impossible to imagine without access to credit. The revolutionary concept here is that micro-credit to the very poorest, without collateral, is not only feasible, it works extremely well.

Poverty and urban environmental degradation go hand in hand, for it is the poor who live in the misery of insanitary conditions. The creation of humane environments and livable cities is within our grasp. No revolutionary new technology is required; we know the methods and have seen them work. The will to implement what we know and the determination to succeed in doing so is what is needed.

In the forty-seven least developed countries of the world, 10 per cent of the world's population subsists on less than 0.5 per cent of the world's income. Some forty thousand people die from hunger-related causes every day. Many of the poor who survive lack access to the fundamental requirements of a decent existence. Over a billion people are compelled to live on less than a dollar a day. A sixth or more of the human race lives a marginalised existence. These conditions can only worsen as the urban populations of the developing countries treble over the coming generation. This is the challenge that lies before us.

Note

1   Ela R Bhatt, 'Financing a Productive House', *Economic Times*, 27 February 1996 (cited in the World Bank booklet, *Livable Cities for the Twenty-First Century*, 1996).

THE NEW LANDSCAPE

Charles Correa

The scale of the problem determines the solution. This is the key to the strategies we must develop over the next twenty-five years. If we succeed in our interventions, then we might actually be able to use the unprecedented growth of cities to our permanent gain, and emerge from the tunnel that lies ahead – so to speak – better off than when we entered. After all, most cities in the past have grown in continuous, incremental stages. Thus the authorities never perceived the opportunity to 'rearrange the scenery'. Let us, for instance, turn the clock back to the time when New York had only one or two million inhabitants. If, at that stage, it was apparent that it would soon have to accommodate ten million people, then a lot of basic structural changes might have been not only financially possible but *politically* viable, and New York today would be a far more rationally organised city.

This, in the final analysis, is the advantage of our predicament. For the first time in history, we are able to perceive an enormous quantum leap in urban growth; a perception that should really prompt us to readjust the scenery we've inherited. Intelligently done, this could have staggering geopolitical implications, for instance, the kind of leverage the USA gets from having an urban structure which spans a continent and connects two oceans. A little over a century ago, the USA was dominated by its eastern seaboard cities (Boston, New York, etc), facing only the Atlantic. The reason why that nation can now address the Pacific is that in the interim there has grown a matching set of urban centres along the West Coast (San Francisco, Los Angeles, etc) and also right across the continent (Detroit, Chicago, Denver). It is an organic, interdependent urban structure generated by the enormous population growth that has taken place in the USA over the last hundred years. In contrast, Australia – a continent which was structured to face Britain through its south-eastern ports of Melbourne and Sydney, though it now suspects that its future lies with its Asian neighbours to the immediate north and west – does not have the dynamic population growth necessary to make such urban restructuring possible. Where there's growth, there's hope.

This is not to say that the population should continue to grow in the Third World. It is merely to emphasise that in spite of anything we do, the population will in many cases double before it stabilises ('Enough girl babies have already

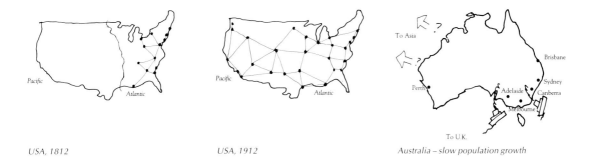

USA, 1812

USA, 1912

Australia – slow population growth

been born, etc . . .'). We do not have much choice about that. What we do have is a choice about patterns of distribution across nations – as well as the internal structuring within the urban centres. Future generations will certainly hold us accountable for missing that unique opportunity.

The colossal numbers involved need neither confuse nor intimidate us. True, a single city of ten million seems unmanageable; but what if the same population is distributed in a poly-centred system, of five or six centres, each of a reasonable size? Such urban structures already exist, for instance in the Bay Area in California where a number of separate centres (San Francisco, Oakland, Marine County, etc) all form one urban system involving over five million people – and yet San Francisco itself has a population of under 900,000. In the same way, several Dutch cities (Amsterdam, The Hague, Rotterdam) together form a single poly-nucleared urban system, each unit of which still possesses a manageable and human scale. And in India Kanpur, Allahabad, Lucknow, etc, form one urban system.

These kinds of models are certainly worth examining. In fact, it is disquieting to realise how seldom we stop to ponder how wide open our options might really be. Perhaps what is needed is not just more towns and cities (in the conventional sense) but a new kind of community which is 'quasi-urban, quasi-rural', one which produces densities high enough to support an educational system and a bus service, yet low enough for each family to keep a buffalo or a goat – and a banana tree. In fact, if one can bring down the residential densities to about fifty households per hectare, it becomes feasible to dispense with central sewage systems and instead recycle waste matter (both human and animal) to considerable advantage – for cooking gas, fertiliser, small vegetable gardens, etc. Under Indian conditions this would have the additional advantage of continuing the pattern of life to which people are accustomed – as though Mahatma Gandhi's vision of a rural India had an almost exact quasi-urban analogue.

Like gobar and biogas, to us in India the sun is, of course, another great harbinger of the new landscape. For much of the Third World, the most cost-effective strategies for harnessing solar energy are not those using gadgets like solar frying pans (expensive to produce and relatively inefficient) but those that set up biological cycles, such as shallow ponds to grow algae and plants which photosynthesise the solar incident on the water and which are then ingested by fish and other higher forms of life, and so forth, until we are the final recipients (though of course, in turn we must inevitably be consumed by something else in order to continue the cycle!). The employment-generating possibilities of such cycles are considerable, as a pilot project in New Bombay demonstrated. Here it was estimated that the building of the ponds would not only provide additional jobs, but also that the excavated soil could be used to form simple sun-dried brick.

Such cycles can create not only the economic basis of communities, but of necessity can also determine their physical pattern – just as today's cities have been generated by the carriage and the automobile. They constitute a new type of human settlement, using the Third World's unique combination of plentiful sunlight and abundant human labour.

If – and when – these settlements come into being, they will bring about two fundamental changes. First, since sunlight falls just about equally over Third World countries, the demographic pattern of population distribution will also follow suit, avoiding the centralisation and the large concentrations inherent in industrialisation. Second, following on from this pattern of evenly distributed self-contained communities, the political power structure must change dramatically, since no one will be able to pull a lever in Delhi (or Lagos, or São Paolo, or Jakarta) and affect millions of people right across the country.

Postulating these profoundly important prototypical settlements for the Third World must go beyond the question of employment; what we need to metamorphosise is the social system, the lifestyle of the new settlements. After all, the communes of Mao are not just a legal contract binding a certain number of people to harvest together, but are really the only political-social human reality the commune members know (like fish know the water they swim in). It will take an effort of equivalent inventiveness to find the *modus operandi* for these new human settlements.

In the past, such imaginative conceptualising was seldom lacking. For instance, in India since Vedic times, sacred diagrams called *mandalas* have formed the basis of architecture and city planning. These square *mandalas*, subdivided in prescribed ratios (from 1 to 1,024 sub-squares), represent a model of the cosmos no less! The hierarchy they generate forms a matrix for locational decisions, whether of deities in a temple, or of the principal buildings in a city. They make explicit a Platonic ideal of built form which in turn reinforces and stabilises society.

Today such concepts are certainly not in current use. Furthermore, it would be foolish to think of invoking them unless we also subscribed to the underlying construct of the cosmos they are meant to represent. Yet, in a century when science has postulated an ever-expanding universe, it may be well worth considering the modelling of our central beliefs as the basis for structuring our environment.

At the other extreme, we must learn to be equally inventive about how we generate our habitat at the micro-scale. For instance, there is little relation between the form of our streets and how we use them. Most pavements in Bombay are

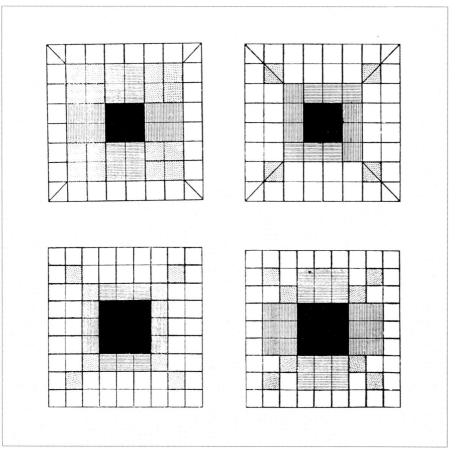

Mandalas: models of the cosmos

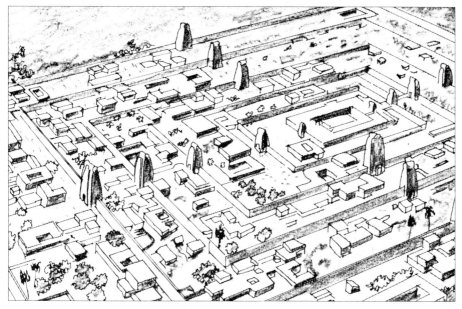

The mandala as temple town – Srirangam, South India

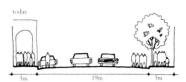

Modifying Bombay's streets with a line of platforms 2 metres wide and 0.5 metres high, with water taps at 30-metre intervals. During the day these platforms would be used by hawkers, thus clearing the arcades for pedestrians. In the evening, water from the taps would wash the platforms clean, creating otlas for people to sleep on.

always crowded – during the day with hawkers (forcing pedestrians onto the traffic lanes), and, as evening falls, with people unfolding their bedding for a night's rest.

These night people are not pavement-dwellers, but mostly domestic servants and office boys who keep their belongings in a shared room, and use city pavements for sleeping at night. This pattern allows them to economise on living expenses (and thus maximise the monthly remittances sent back to their villages). What is dismaying is not that they sleep outdoors (on hot sultry nights, obviously a more attractive proposition than a crowded airless room), but that they have to do so in unhygienic conditions, with the public walking right amongst (and over!) them. Is there any way the city streets and pavements could respond to their needs?

To be involved in these issues, the architect will have to act not as a prima donna professional, but as one who is willing to donate his energy – and his ideas – to society. It is a role that has a very important historic precedent. For throughout most of Asia, his prototype in the past was the site *mistri*, an experienced mason/carpenter who helped with the design and construction of the habitat. Even today in the small towns and villages of India, the practice continues. Owner and *mistri* go together to the site, and with a stick scratch into the earth the outline of the building they wish to construct. There is some argument back and forth about the relative advantages of various window positions, stairways, and so forth. But the system works because both builder and user share the same aesthetic, they are both on the same side of the table! It was exactly this kind of equation that produced the great architecture of the past, from Chartres to the Alhambra to Fatehpur-Sikri. (If the architect today cannot win an argument with a company executive, would he have been able to overrule a Moghul Emperor three hundred years ago – and survived?)

Today, the situation is quite different. Not only has the shared aesthetic evaporated, but the interface has diminished. Only about 10 per cent of the population has the resources to commission the kind of buildings the academically trained architect has learned to design – and only a tenth of them would think of engaging him (the others would appoint a civil engineer, or perhaps a contractor directly). So there you have the architect's interface with society: all of 1 per cent. This figure represents the people who commission the office buildings,

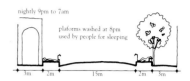

apartments, luxury hotels, factories and houses that make up the bulk of the architect's practice. The situation is not of his making; it merely reflects the grotesque inequality within society itself. But of course it is the poor whose needs are the most desperate. Today, in Rio or Lagos or Calcutta, there are millions living in illegal squatter colonies. Is the architect, with his highly specialised skills, going to find a way to be of any relevance to them?

Unfortunately, even among those architects who have enough of a social conscience to want to reach out to the poor, many are really a-visual – in fact, in some cases, belligerently *anti-visual* – rejoicing (as they move among the poor like Florence Nightingale among the wounded) in the acres of ugliness/goodness of it all. What these communities need is not just our compassion, but our professional (ie: visual and topological) skills. Without these, the squatter colonies will turn out to be nightmares – proliferating, over the next two decades, on a mind-boggling scale. In turn, they will maim whole generations of Third World children, condemned to grow up in such environments.

We cannot just trust to luck and a blind faith in humanity; for every Mykonos history has created, there are ten other depressing towns. The stunningly beautiful handicraft and weaving of certain societies are the (fortunate) result of a cumulative process, spread out over many decades – each generation making marginal improvements to the end-product. Without the benefit of such a heritage to provide context, people often opt for ugly things (it is the principle of Miami Beach); if we want to increase the probability of winding up with something as beautiful as Udaipur, then strategies for sites-and-services will have to be programmed accordingly. Perhaps extra weight should also be given to those of the inhabitants who are more visually sensitive, so as to hasten the process. (In a self-help scheme in New Bombay, for instance, folk artists were brought in as catalysts, to work with the householders.)

To value the visual component, so obviously present in traditional habitat, is not to join the enthusiasms of today's fashionable eclecticism. Far from it. We must understand our past well enough to value it, yet also well enough to know why (and how) it must be changed. Architecture is not just a reinforcement of existing values – social, political, economic. On the contrary. It should open new doors to new aspirations.

To reach the millions who lie on the pavements and in the shanty towns is to get involved in a whole new series of issues; issues to which we must bring the instincts – and the skills – of the architect. I emphasise this again, because too often, in entering this arena, the architect leaves the best of himself behind. Hence the stultifying sites-and-services schemes – all 'justified' on the grounds that an aesthetic sense is something the poor cannot afford.

Nothing, of course, could be further from the truth. Improving the habitat needs visual skills. The poor have always understood this. With one stroke of a pink brush, a Mexican artisan transforms a clay pot. It costs him nothing, but it can change your life. It is not a coincidence that the best handicraft comes from the poorest countries of this world – Nepal, Mexico and India, for example. And the Arab had only the simplest of resources – mud and sun – so he *had* to be inventive, and in the process produced some of the most glorious oasis towns (low-energy, high-visual) the world has ever seen. From the Polynesian Islands to the Mediterranean hill-towns to the Jungles of Assam, for thousands of years people have been building beautiful habitats.

In fact, if we look at all the fashionable concerns of environmentalists today – balanced ecosystems, recycling waste products, appropriate lifestyles, indigenous technology – we find that the people of the Third World already have it all. Ironically enough, that's the wonderful thing about the Third World: there is no shortage of housing. What there is a shortage of, most definitely, is the urban context in which these marvellously inventive solutions are viable. This then is our prime responsibility: to help generate that urban context.

Architecture as an agent of change – which is why a leader like Mahatma Gandhi is called the Architect of the Nation, not the Engineer, or the Dentist, or the Historian. The architect is the generalist who speculates on how the pieces could fit together in more advantageous ways; one who is concerned with what well might be.

To do this, in the context of the Third World, the architect must have the courage to face disturbing issues. For what is your moral right to decide for ten thousand, for a hundred thousand, for two million people? But then what is the moral advantage in not acting, in merely watching passively the slow degradation of life around you?

This is indeed a cruel dilemma: to act or not to act? On the one hand, the dangers of fascism, on the other the paralysis of Hamlet. It is a profoundly disturbing issue, and one which will define the key moral values of the first half of the twenty-first century. In this, the role of the architect will be central: can we really understand another's aspirations? In the 1960s, when European hippies first started coming to Bombay, a lot of rich Indians complained bitterly about them. At dinner parties they would refer to those 'terrible, dirty people, with lice in their hair, lying on the pavements begging'. In response one would say: 'It doesn't bother you when you see a European?' Finally, a friend gave me the answer: 'Naturally a rich Indian goes berserk when he drives his Mercedes and sees a hippie. The hippie is signalling him a message: "I'm confused where

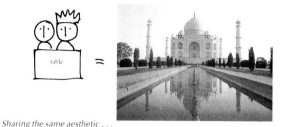

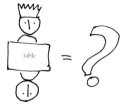

Sharing the same aesthetic . . . *. . . as opposed to conning the client*

you're going – and it's not worth going there." That upsets him terribly.' But come to think of it, surely it is a message that should work the other way around as well. The hippie should realise that the Indian in his Mercedes, gross as he may be, is also sending a message, in fact, the very same one: 'I'm coming from where you're going.'

We are but ships that pass in the night – as a photograph of Bombay's skyline illustrates so poignantly. Silhouetted in the foreground are the squatters. Behind them rise new skyscrapers. To us the buildings are ugly and deplorable – but to them they form the surreal, mythic image of the city which they yearn for, but which they may never attain.

A twentieth-century composer – I think it was Hindemith – was once asked the mind-boggling question: 'How do you compose music?' To which he gave an astonishingly evocative answer: 'It is like looking out of a window into the black night of a thunderstorm. Suddenly there is a flash of lightning, illuminating the entire landscape. In that one split second, one has seen everything – and nothing. What is called composition is the patient recreation of that landscape, stone by stone, tree by tree.'

Will the cities of the Third World survive the next few decades? The answer may well depend on whether or not we have the perspicacity to search out and recognise the stones and trees as they gradually coalesce into the new landscape.

This essay was first published in Charles Correa, The New Landscape, *Book Club of India, Bombay, 1985, pp119-35. Reprinted by Concept Media (Singapore), 1988.*

CONVERGENCE, MARGINALISATION AND INEQUALITY

DIRECTIONS FOR THE URBAN FUTURE

Michael Cohen

Defining the Problem

The increasing inequality between rich and poor countries, within countries, and within cities and towns is one of the most important socio-economic determinants of our future. The 1996 UNDP Human Development Report once again describes the patterns of increasing inequality. Despite the relatively good economic performance of some developing countries, the gap between the developed and developing countries has increased. What is the role of cities in this process? Have the disparities between cities also increased? Have they been reduced or increased by the forces of globalisation?

The Hypothesis of Urban Convergence

In 1995, I posed the 'hypothesis of urban convergence' in a discussion on how urban settlements had changed since the Vancouver Conference of 1976. The hypothesis stated that the most important features of cities in developing and developed countries were becoming more similar.[1] These converging features were declining infrastructure, deteriorating urban environment, growing unemployment, fraying social cohesion, and institutional weakness. While the meaning and origins of these problems vary between countries and between urban areas within countries, they nevertheless represent a shared set of challenges which face city authorities. The most serious aspects of these problems can be summarised as follows:

Declining Infrastructure: Cities in both developed and developing countries face severe problems in the operation and maintenance of existing infrastructure stock such as water supply, sanitation, transportation and waste treatment. Pressures on existing networks and distribution systems are exacerbated by growing demand for both the quantity and quality of services, particularly in fast-growing urban areas in developing countries, but also in developed countries where changing urban spatial patterns require additional new investments.

Deteriorating Urban Environment: The overall decline in the quality of air, water and land resources in most cities in the world is shared by both developed and developing countries. Even if data from Europe and North America shows improved environmental quality during the 1990s, this applies to only privileged centres within those countries. The 1996 World Resource Report provides excellent data on the shared experiences of most cities.[2] Moreover, the data demonstrates the likelihood of a Kuznets curve of environmental quality, ie: as national and urban incomes increase, environmental quality may deteriorate as a result of increased activity in the absence of strengthened environmental management.

Growing Urban Unemployment: The demographic bases of unemployment differ from developing to developed countries, with the former expanding due to high birth rates and growing numbers of potential entrants into the labour force, and the latter reflecting the rapid growth of female labour-force participation and the impact of technologies on the demand for labour. Yet, both types of society face the problem of increasing demand for jobs, with the resulting social tensions and frustrated aspirations.

Fraying Social Cohesion: The prospects of differential access to job and income-earning opportunities are powerful forces in generating social tension between groups of all kinds. If the realities of international migration, disasters and severe ethnic problems are added together, it should not be surprising that urban social tensions are manifest in most societies. Fifteen of the twenty poorest developing countries have experienced serious civil unrest over the last decade.

Institutional Weakness: These problems cumulatively place intense pressures on already weak urban institutions which have neither the financial nor the technical capacities to solve the problems facing them. Processes of decentralisation have more frequently meant the devolution of responsibility for problem-solving to local levels than the true decentralisation of resources needed to address these problems. Whether viewed as resulting from 'unfunded mandates' or 'phantom decentralisation', weak urban institutional capacity remains perhaps the major shared problem of cities in both developing and developed countries.

While the objective realities of these problems are surprisingly similar, their origins and meanings differ between cities. Curiously, all cities and towns strenuously assert their special character in a 'resurgent localism', arguing that their own people in their own place makes them different from any other community. This special character of each locality is an important part of the empowerment process because it is frequently the assertion of difference which is politically and psychologically important in local mobilisation.

Yet, I believe that the assertion of local character by every community is another example of urban convergence. If everyone is doing it, they are converging!

Globalisation of the Virtual City

The shared problems facing cities are also affected by the dynamic features of the global economy and the information society. Several aspects of globalisation deserve special mention:

— The changing composition of transactions between countries from trade to international flows has resulted in dramatic increases in foreign direct investment – three times faster than trade – during the last decade.

— As foreign direct investment has grown, the share of local economic activity which is in fact 'delocalised', linked to components and production processes out of the local areas, has grown many times.

— The resulting changes in patterns of ownership of land and other urban assets, including infrastructure, units of production, and services, are reflected in new spatial patterns, what Saskia Sassen calls a 'new geography of centres and margins'.

— If the information distance in this geography has been reduced, the disparities in economic and financial power have grown.

The most critical consequence of these processes has been rapidly changing structures of opportunity and competition. Cities connected to the new networks are included in the flow of information and capital, while those outside the networks – in Africa and other poor areas – are experiencing marginalisation.

These cities, such as Dar es Salaam and Bamako, are not only not included in global economic and information processes, but they find themselves in the downward spiral of inequality cited above. They fall faster and faster behind, with foreign private investment seeking nodes of activity, not the ends of the line. They do not experience the schizophrenia of the 'virtual city', living in environments heavily affected by daily changes in the global economy and appearing on computer screens. Rather, they are rooted in the muddy streets of the status quo.

Urban Marginalisation within Economic Communities

This phenomenon is particularly interesting when considered in light of the new trading blocs such as MERCOSUR or APEC. The differences in trading opportunities for members of APEC, for example Japan and Indonesia, directly reflect differences in urban infrastructure and institutional capacity. The annual operating budget of the Municipality of Osaka alone in 1994 was US$50 billion, many times larger than all of the combined budgets of all the cities and towns of Indonesia. It is not surprising that many of the weaker nations and localities within these trading blocs are becoming alarmed by the prospect of being unable to attract footloose private investment and being left behind in the competition for jobs and income.

These global economic processes, therefore, are both directly related to local urban conditions and have an impact on them. The threat of unequal opportunity and marginalisation is real for cities. This suggests that the apparent convergence of important features of urban areas may be transitory if cities are unable to marshal the capacity to address these problems. The downside risk of 'think globally, act locally' is that failed local action will affect global thinking about specific places.

Notes

1   Cohen et al, *Preparing for the Urban Future: Global Pressures and Local Forces*, John Hopkins University Press (Baltimore), 1996.

2   World Resource Report, World Resources Institute (Washington), 1996.

ARCHITECTURE TO CHANGE THE WORLD?

Suha Özkan

Even in today's so-called information society, there is no practical possibility of determining what percentage of the built environment is being shaped by architects as members of a responsible profession. We still refer to C Doxiadis's assertion, made in the mid-1960s, that 98 per cent of the built environment is shaped without any professional intervention by architects.[1] Since then, given the demand for building from rapidly growing populations, the percentage can only have increased.

The rapid urbanisation in the 1960s in the cities of the Third World was only passively observed by those who were 'responsible for' offering solutions. The professionals and politicians had engaged themselves in endless rhetoric while the previously insignificant towns grew into mega-cities with the influx of massive populations. The problem grew to such proportions that everyone started to talk about the threshold of an explosion.

In the beginning, and with all good intentions, the architectural profession meant to solve these problems by architectural means. The understanding was that since these were problems of building, solutions would obviously lie within the scope of architecture and could be managed by design. Technology-intensive methods were based on a building tradition that had been disrupted by changes in technology during the period of modernisation. The reinstatement of traditional technologies, which were still alive and practised in various sectors of society, especially in rural areas, was seemingly a rational approach.

Hassan Fathy was the pioneer who challenged all of the materials, construction methods and technologies that were not local. His architecture, though directed at the poor, had the support of many of the upper classes who supported the development of an indigenous culture. In order to display the validity of his architecture, Fathy did not hesitate to build for the rich. However, his discourse[2] and architecture could not achieve their intended result of harmonious living imbued with cultural values and historical continuity. This was because they were based on traditional methods and modes of building at the very time when the Egyptian communities he was building for were undergoing radical transformation. Fathy's technical solutions were rendered irrelevant by changes in societal values. He did, indeed, produce many elegant individual residences,

 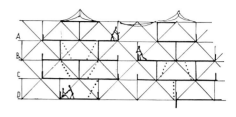

Yona Friedman, African Proposals, 1959 (courtesy of Yona Friedman)

but his efforts at social housing, such as in the village of New Gourna, alas were a failure. The solution to the problem of a 'new' human habitat in urban areas was not technological, but social and economic. It is here that some of Fathy's pioneering thinking, if not his application of it, remains valid. As Ismaïl Serageldin noted in his evaluation of Fathy:

> In the final analysis Hassan Fathy's contribution to Egyptian architecture has been his image-faculty, his ability to give body and form to a concept that was always recognised but that could not be easily seen . . . In the realm of ideas his emphasis on self-help, concern for the poor, cultural authenticity and individualism are now so widely accepted that it is difficult to remember the revolutionary character of his message when he enunciated it so long ago. It is an impressive legacy.[3]

On a different scale, Yona Friedman was also professing solutions based on technology. In *Une utopie réalisée*, he proposed contemporary or even futurist technology which offered people the alternative of constructing their own homes.[4] The multi-layered space truss that he proposed was capable of accommodating all necessary infrastructure, and therefore provided people with the freedom to build in any configuration of their choice which they could afford. Obviously, these visions sought to bring control to housing.

In Fathy's case, the technical solution was the centuries-old tradition of building; in Friedman's, it was a container of amenities that provided environmental and infrastructural standards, while social relationships were left for individuals to determine themselves. Courageously, he proposed this thesis as a means of coping with the *bidonvilles* in Algeria. Many other solutions were proposed by other architects, and almost all of them responded to the global humanist concerns of the time. Architects sought to offer their professional skills – through the means of architectural technology – to help relieve the pains of rapid urbanisation.

In the 1970s, architectural discourse was enriched by quite a variety of new movements or 'isms', all of which highlighted certain aspects of architecture that were either missing in the one-dimensional architectural approach, or were not particularly fashionable within the then-prevailing ethos of the profession.

Vernacular architecture, Yemen   *Vernacular architecture, Sidi bou Said, Tunis*

Vernacularism gave priority to the traditional modes of building which had been tested and sustained throughout history, and which therefore could not be wrong. Bernard Rudolfsky ironically coined the term 'architecture without architects' for this mode of building.[5] Increasing interest in research led to a more complex, societal understanding of architectural phenomena, especially as related to housing.

Fathy's disciples were committed to, and even more adventurous in developing, 'an architecture *of* the site', as opposed to the architectural ideal of 'an architecture *on* the site'. These young architects established an approach on the premise of Fathy's idiom: 'Wherever human beings live, there are materials indigenous to the locale to offer solutions for their shelter'. Thus, approaches using alternative technologies gained momentum. Groups like the Development Workshop (London), ADAUA (Geneva), CRATerre (Grenoble) and many others, dedicated their careers to the development of indigenous technologies which are environmentally friendly. All these groups, organised primarily around these architectural ideals, sought solutions by means of architecture, and therefore by technology. They concentrated their efforts in rural areas, whereas it was informal building in urban areas that was quickly growing out of control.

It became apparent that the introduction of solutions which did not take people's own preferences into account led to their rejection or, at best, only partial acceptance. For example, a substantial amount of government-provided housing has remained unoccupied in Turkey; and in Egypt, people radically changed and adapted such housing to better suit their own needs and desires. Whether this should be called 'disfiguration' or 'adaptation' is debatable, but the fact remains that the architect's approach was either rejected or transformed. It was at this point that 'participation' entered forcefully into architectural discourse as a viable alternative, one which allowed users to project their own desires and ideals.

Participationism challenged the idea of the omnipotent architect who was supposed to know everything about people's needs and, accordingly, be able to provide for them.[6] The notion arose that solutions determined by architectural decisions were not necessarily those which people needed, wanted, or were

A residence by Hassan Fathy, Cairo, Egypt

Social housing by CRATerre, Mayotte, Comoro Islands

Literacy Centre by ADAUA, Nouakchott, Mauritania

Plaster housing by ADAUA, Nouakchott, Mauritania

comfortable with. Subsequently, the involvement of users in architecture took various forms. Some provided networks of infrastructure in order to let people build their own houses. Others tried to predetermine needs by questionnaires, so that the end product would be based upon and fit these needs. (This approach was radicalised by the Belgian architect Lucien Kroll into the concept of an 'architecture of anarchy'.) Needless to say, the liberation of individual users from the dominating egos of architects not only provided better solutions for housing, but also culminated in novel expressions of contemporary architecture.

The provision of industrial technology also allowed people to employ 'ready-made' mechanisms (for example, 'do-it-yourself' or 'self-help' housing) to solve their own needs and problems. With the exception of fire hazards, people mainly needed outside advice on the mechanical and structural determinants of building, however primitive they might be introduced in 'self-made' environments. ('Mobile homes', in many respects, worked within the same parameters, although this solution remained marginal.) Nevertheless, for most people, the architecturally important part seemed to be the concept of 'home'; the most important aspects were economic and communal. Thus, jobs, and access to communal facilities, were more important determinants than sound shelter.

In Charles Jencks' and Nathan Silver's provoking book entitled *Adhocism*,[7] the validity of creative, individualised solutions was introduced into architectural discourse. This was more in line with Christopher Alexander's 'unselfconscious' design, where solutions were derived from resources driven by need, instead of through formalised ideals.

The current information revolution has introduced the possibility of decentralised urban settings, by letting people work outside the urban centres. However, this is not yet the case for the majority of less-educated people employed in the service sector. Proximity to the work place remains essential. Charles Correa based his plan for New Bombay on the premise that people do not come to cities for urban life, but for jobs. Therefore, the distribution of employment determines housing needs. In this respect, Correa has powerfully demonstrated that, instead of stacking people up in housing blocks, if they are given the possibility of direct access to the ground, they will develop better communal relationships, and will also develop their own homes much more freely and economically.

Many others, like Muhammad Yunus of the Grameen Bank, and Tasneem Ahmad Siddiqui of the Hyderabad Development Authority, see housing not as a primary concern, but as the natural product of decent living. Therefore, the economic empowerment of people to develop their own physical environments with limited help from others is the most important aspect. Because a home is a natural need, and because people's images of their own homes are structured by their economic situation, these planners have studied the vicious circle of the existing credit mechanisms and, instead, have developed a model of providing credit which permits human dignity and communal commitment. Their models provided excellent solutions, leading to recognition by the Aga Khan Award for

Architecture. Since these projects redefined architecture not around the ideals of the profession, but around the concepts of social and economic well-being, their architectural solutions have been the minimum sufficient to provide what was needed. Is this not one of the basic principles of Modernism too?

In his trend-setting book *Freedom to Build*,[8] John FC Turner professed the need to liberate societies from the dominating forces outside the control of the distorted ideals of profession and bureaucracy, both of which have a self-confirming logic which is never a solution for individuals. There have been many examples in the past of people who were victimised by war or natural disasters seeking help in the form of credit as opposed to housing provisions. The availability of credit, either in kind – especially in rural areas in the form of materials – or in cash, offers the freedom of selecting the communal setting in which people would like to live. The provision and distribution of housing with random and arbitrary allocation brings less healthy, imposed societal relationships which very seldom work. Access to building materials and technological know-how, and allowing people to determine the configuration, siting and spaces of their own homes, leads to a technology-dominated architectural harmony. In most cases, this harmony relieves the sharper, irritating expressions of imposed architecture, and permits more modest and humane environments.

Architects who have tried to pursue this role of enabler, to empower the people to take charge, have had consistent recognition from the various juries of the Aga Khan Award for Architecture. It is time that many more people recognise the quality of their powerful if discreet and subtle role. Their practice is what Ismaïl Serageldin has aptly called the 'Architecture of Empowerment'.

Notes

'Architecture to Change the World' was a notion formulated by the Moroccan architect Elie Mouyal to convey his understanding of the mission and objective which the Aga Khan Award for Architecture has created for itself.

1   Constantin Dioxiadis, *Architecture in Transition*, Hutchinson (London), 1963.

2   Hassan Fathy, *Architecture for the Poor*, University of Chicago Press (Chicago), 1973.

3   Ismaïl Serageldin, 'An Egyptian Appraisal', in James M Richards, Ismaïl Serageldin and Darl Rastorfer, *Hassan Fathy*, Mimar Books (Singapore), 1985, pp23-24.

4   Yona Friedman, *Une utopie réalisée*, Museum of Modern Art (New York), 1975.

5   Bernard Rudolfsky, *Architecture without Architects*, Museum of Modern Art (New York), 1964.

6   Giancarlo de Carlo, *The Architecture of Participation*, Royal Institute of Architects (Melbourne), 1972; Nigel Cross, *Design Participation: Proceedings of the Design Research Society Conference, Manchester*, Academy Editions (London), 1972.

7   Charles Jencks and Nathan Silver, *Adhocism: A Case for Improvisation*, Secker and Warburg (London), 1972.

8   John FC Turner and R Fichter, *Freedom to Build*, Macmillan (New York) 1972.

REDEEMING THE LEGACY OF THE PAST

Whether rich or poor, people value their identity. In many cities of the developing world, the historic centres have now become home to the poorest citizens. They are concentrated here by the force of economic and land-use policies that have resulted in a daily confrontation between the search for a better life and the need to conserve and transform a priceless architectural and urban heritage. Three case studies dealing with Bukhara in Uzbekistan, Sana'a in Yemen, and Lamu in Kenya show how the key to success lies in involving the local community and in utilising the best technical knowledge possible. Respecting the past – while transforming it for the needs of the present and responding to the needs of the people – is the way to redeem its legacy.

CONSERVATION OF OLD SANA'A
SANA'A, YEMEN

Mohammad al-Asad and Ismaïl Serageldin

Sana'a is located on the central mountain plateau of Yemen, over 2,500 metres above sea level. It was founded about two thousand years ago, and has always been an important political and economic centre for south-western Arabia. Closed to foreign influence for over two hundred years until 1962, the city retains its pre-modern character to a degree not found in most other cities.

Sana'a's architectural heritage is well known and the subject of numerous studies. It is regarded as a unique part of the world heritage and efforts for its conservation are under way. But it has problems: the new city surrounding the old centre is growing quickly, and the dense and special character of the old architecture is not easily adaptable to some modern amenities. The challenge to the planners was to restore the architectural character, to involve the local community, foreign financiers and the private sector; and to keep work under the control of the local population, which was represented by a special Yemeni office called the General Organisation for the Preservation of the Historic Cities of Yemen (GOPHCY). Since its foundation in 1984, GOPHCY has had difficulties living up to the promise of its mandate, despite having had a

dynamic chief of restoration in Abdallah Hadrami. In order to address the problems faced by the old city, GOPHCY has had to work in association with UNESCO, UNDP and the governments of Italy, The Netherlands, North Korea, Norway, South Korea, Switzerland, France and the United States of America, as well as the local inhabitants and various Yemeni agencies. The challenge to co-ordinate all these participants while keeping a clear Yemeni 'ownership' of the enterprise was a daunting one, and one that has only partially been met in practice. Nevertheless, the achievements of the programme are noteworthy and warrant attention in this discussion of protecting the legacy of the past.

The old city is famous for its highly decorated multi-storey structures which rise to as many as nine storeys. Along with the tall minarets of the city's mosques, they define a city skyline that leaves an unforgettable impression.

The ground level of the typical house in old Sana'a usually consists of stables. The two storeys above it contain reception areas. The remaining storeys, except for the uppermost one, are all reserved for the living quarters. The uppermost storey, the *mafraj*, has commanding views and is

View of the old town of Sana'a, Yemen

A multi-storey house typical of old Sana'a

Bayt Sari, a richly decorated facade typical of old Sana'a

open on three sides. It functions as a reception area where the owner of the house receives guests in the afternoon.

The lower levels are usually built of stone, and the upper ones of lighter brick. The windows are outlined in white gypsum and have fan lights of alabaster or coloured glass held in gypsum tracery. The main door opens onto a central stairway which connects the various storeys. These stairs wrap around a massive column. This column acts as the main structural member of the building and forms a support to which most of the beams of the structure connect.

The intensive land use made possible by these tall buildings frees considerable areas of the city for agricultural purposes. In fact, old Sana'a has a significant amount of green areas used as orchards and vegetable gardens.

GOPHCY – and the international and foreign organisations that have aided it – began its campaign to safeguard old Sana'a by carrying out a series of technical studies addressing the challenges facing the city. These studies were then turned into actual projects, some of which relied exclusively on Yemeni skills and funding, others on foreign technical and financial assistance.

These projects have addressed old Sana'a at both urban and architectural levels. On the urban level, the city's infrastructure has been upgraded and its streets and passageways paved. The infrastructure programme was carried out between 1987 and 1988, and was funded and executed by the Yemeni government. It included improving the old water supply and drainage systems that were installed after the 1962 revolution.

The paving project, also started and financed by the Yemeni government, has effectively dealt with problems of dust and mud. The use of black and white stone has also enhanced the appearance of the streets. About 50 per cent of the old city's streets and passageways have been paved. Funding for the continuation of this project has been provided by many foreign donors.

Other urban-scale projects include the preservation and restoration of the city's southern wall; of the Wadi Sa'ilah, which is the flood course that crosses the city from north to south; and of the vegetable gardens.

On the architectural level, a considerable number of buildings have been restored in old Sana'a and nearby areas such as Bir al-'Azab and Rawdah. The first building which GOPHCY restored was Dar al-Jadid, which was constructed in the mid-seventeenth century with subsequent additions made in the mid-twentieth century. It was deserted when renovation work began in 1987. Renovation work was funded by the Yemeni government and was completed in 1989 and, since then, the structure has served as the headquarters of GOPHCY. In addition to Dar al-Jadid, a few dozen buildings have been renovated in the Sana'a area since the late 1980s, some by GOPHCY or in co-ordination with it, others by the private sector.

Samsarat al-Mansurah, top of the open stairwell leading to the terrace

Numerous vegetable gardens and orchards punctuate the dense urban fabric

Samsarat al-Nuhas which now houses a craft training centre

The private-sector renovations carried out in old Sana'a can be divided into two main groups: hotels and private residences. The cost of renovating the private houses has been successfully passed on by the Yemeni owners to the mainly foreign tenants. Most of these structures were built between the mid-eighteenth and mid-twentieth centuries. On the whole, renovation has taken place between 1987 and the present in consultation with Abdallah Hadrami.

Most projects have shown considerable sensitivity to the traditional architectural features of Sana'a, as well as incorporating traditional materials and construction techniques. Another positive feature is that both Yemenis and non-Yemenis have collaborated on their design and execution. This joining of the skills of local architects and craftsmen with those of foreign architectural conservators has been very fruitful. As a result of their collaborative efforts, Sana'a now has Yemeni architects, engineers and craftsmen who can competently carry out renovation work to international standards.

Before discussing the socio-economic effects of this project on life in old Sana'a, it should be mentioned that no exact data is available on the socio-economic make-up of the city. It is estimated that the inhabitants of old Sana'a amount to about seventy thousand. A number of the original inhabitants have remained; though a good number of them, especially the wealthier ones, have left the city for newer parts of Sana'a where hygiene levels and services are of a better quality. People of a lower socio-economic background, many rural immigrants, have moved to old Sana'a to take their place. Consequently, the socio-economic composition of the traditional city, and the diversity which it expressed, has diminished during the past few years.

The paving project has definitely revitalised those parts of the city which it has affected. In residential areas, it has often resulted in the ground level of houses being converted from stables into shops. This development has had mixed results: while it has brought life back to these neighbourhoods, it has also brought them more pedestrian and vehicular traffic than they

can handle. In this context, it is interesting to observe that a number of the unpaved parts of the city seem deserted in comparison with the paved ones. In addition to the transport problem, careful action needs to be taken to deal with litter and waste management. A citizen campaign is being launched to involve the city's inhabitants in dealing with these matters.

On the architectural level, the renovated buildings housing development or cultural projects, such as Samsarat al-Nuhas, Samsarat al-Mansurah and Bayt Mutahhar, provide the inhabitants of the old city with services that make a positive contribution to their quality of life. The craft training centres also make significant contributions to preserving the traditional crafts of the area and to providing employment opportunities for inhabitants of the old city. In spite of the cultural and economic importance of such projects, however, they remain just the beginning of the broader effort that is needed to really transform the quality of life in old Sana'a.

In recognition of this major effort by a very poor country struggling with difficult domestic and economic circumstances, the restoration of old Sana'a received an Aga Khan Award for Architecture in 1995. The Jury citation commended it:

For having successfully incorporated the efforts of the public and private sectors, local and foreign bodies, and individuals and groups in protecting one of the jewels of Muslim architectural and urban heritage. The focus on streets and infrastructure, as well as gardens and individual buildings, is noteworthy in an enterprise confronting a living city with a rapidly evolving socio-economic structure.

It is to be hoped that, encouraged by this international recognition, Abdallah Hadrami and the public authorities, working with the citizens of Sana'a, will continue to collaborate with international bodies without being disempowered; with every passing day, they should become more empowered in dealing with the city's problems and more successful at preserving its unique character.

CONSERVATION OF LAMU
LAMU, KENYA

Ismaïl Serageldin

The Swahili city-state of Lamu, off the northern coast of present-day Kenya, was probably founded in the fourteenth century by Arab traders. By the fifteenth century it was a flourishing mercantile centre frequented by both Arab and Persian traders. Portuguese domination of Indian Ocean trade in the sixteenth century witnessed some decline in Lamu's importance, but a revival took place under Omani protection in the seventeenth century. Transfer of the seat of the Omani Sultanate to Zanzibar in 1840 assured new prosperity, and during this time the encouragement of Indian merchants to settle introduced yet another element in the mixture of cultures. By the nineteenth century, German and British spheres of influence had been established and, in 1895, Lamu became part of the East Africa Protectorate administered by the British. Up until this time, the trade and transport of ivory and slaves made up the community's principal sources of income, along with agriculture (mangroves) which was also entirely reliant on slave labour. The abolition of slavery and the increasing importance of Nairobi, on the mainland, and Mombasa, on the coast, further threatened Lamu's existence, and by the early part of this century, the town had become an obscure and almost forgotten port in full economic decline.

Present-day Lamu has a population of twelve thousand. The town is made up of two distinct parts which originally reflected a difference of social and economic status. At the centre and along the seafront are large stone houses and mosques of coral limestone. These are surrounded by an expanding ring of mud, wattle and *makuti* (palm thatch) houses. The stone town, which largely retains its original structure, displays the successive influence of a variety of immigrants and of building styles which continued uninterrupted over a period of five centuries. The remoteness of the area and the absence of roads and vehicles on the island are amongst the factors that have led to the survival of the old town virtually untouched. In recent years, population growth and changing standards, and the decay and neglect of the building stock have posed new threats, augmented by an inadequate infrastructure and the menace of new construction and materials and radical alterations.

It is in response to these conditions that the Lamu Conservation Project was launched. It consists of four main elements: a detailed study

The stone houses of Lamu constitute a beautiful and harmonious seafront

of the architectural as well as the social fabric and economic structure of the historic old town; the establishment of a comprehensive conservation plan which includes national and local legislation, planning policies and design guidelines; demonstration projects focusing on the rehabilitation and improvement of public spaces and buildings; and the active involvement of the local community, including training programmes for the restoration and maintenance of the building stock.

It is this last item that makes the Lamu project notable amongst conservation work in Africa. It was launched under the auspices of the National Museums of Kenya and the Ministry of Lands and Settlements. The overall scheme started with an initial inventory of historic buildings undertaken in 1975, in an effort to foster conservation and to focus public attention on the need to protect the area. Following legislation enacted by the Kenyan Government in 1983 to provide the legal framework to safeguard monuments and places of historical interest, a comprehensive conservation plan was finalised in 1985. This was made up of three distinct parts: detailed planning policies, including local building and land-use regulations, and special measures for the protection of the historical

features of the town; a number of special projects and recommendations to upgrade services and public areas in the town; and building guidelines which give practical guidance to owners and builders making repairs or alterations to old buildings or constructing new houses in the historical area.

Administrative procedures have been developed and will be enforced by a Local Planning Commission (whose members include health, architectural and conservation experts, and members of the local community) through the offices of the City Council. Throughout the programme, great care has been taken to learn and address the needs and aspirations of the local community, and to marry these with analysis of economic viability and technical expertise.

The Lamu project is a landmark effort in Kenya, the first comprehensive conservation plan to have been developed and enacted. Beyond its significance for the local community, it represents a pioneering step towards the recognition and protection of the cultural heritage of the East African Coast.

(Based on information provided by the Aga Khan Award for Architecture's library and documentation services.)

The larger buildings in the centre of the town are different to the makuti *houses at the fringe*

Restoration involves local craftsmen using traditional methods

The architectural character is reflected in the detailing

RESTORATION OF OLD BUKHARA
BUKHARA, UZBEKISTAN

Selma al-Radi

The old town of Bukhara conjures up magical images by its very name. Although it was already a town in the first millennium BC, it became important historically in the eighth century AD, when it was conquered by the Abbasid caliphate (AD709). Bukhara flourished both intellectually and commercially, and by the tenth century AD, under the powerful Samanid Dynasty, it became a renowned centre of the arts and of learning, especially the sciences and mathematics. The city's rich cultural heritage, commissioned by the generous patronage of its rulers, includes many architectural landmarks of the Islamic world, including the Samanid Mausoleum and the Kalyan Minaret. For the last twenty-five years Bukhara has been engaged in an active and successful policy to restore and revitalise the old town with its many monuments.

With a total population of 350,000, Bukhara is situated on the edge of the Kizil Kum desert and has a dry and arid climate. Summers are hot with temperatures that can rise above 40 degrees Centigrade in July, while winters range from -23 to 20 degrees Centigrade. Winds can be ferocious: cold in winter and blowing hard sand in summer. The Zerashan River, once a tributary

of the Amu Darya, used to flow near the town and once supplied water, via the Shahrud Canal, for its canals and pools. These were drained under the Soviet regime, as they carried diseases (especially gastric and skin diseases) and the canals became refuse dumps. A new drainage system was installed.

The overall impression of old Bukhara is of brick – the surrounds are brick-coloured and all the monuments are built of brick. The low skyline of two to three storeys is only interrupted by the tall minarets of the mosques. Only sections of the town wall and two gates have survived – the rest was destroyed when new roads were cut through the town. New Bukhara, with its brutal-looking concrete high-rises, its hotels and government buildings of the Soviet period, surrounds the old town on all sides.

The restoration of single monuments in Bukhara started in the 1920s, but the restoration programme for the old town began during the early 1970s under the USSR. The main reason was to attract tourists and hard currency. Since independence in 1990, Uzbekistan has been redefining its identity and image, and the preservation and reintegration of its cultural and

The Labi-Haus pool in front of the Nadir Divan Begi Madrasa

Street trading in front of the Chashma-Ayub Mausoleum

Street leading to the restored Taq-i Tilpak Furushan in which many shops have opened

The restored Mir-i Arab Madrasa is now used for teaching Islamic studies

The courtyard of the restored Kalyan Mosque

Ceiling of the Abdul Aziz-Khan Madrasa which is now the headquarters of the Bukhara Restoration Office

Glazed tiles on the restored Nadir Divan Begi Madrasa which now houses craft centres and ateliers

architectural heritage is an important component of this policy. Bukhara became the capital of a province. The town is officially celebrating its 2,500th anniversary in 1997, and UNESCO is hosting the celebrations.

The objective of the Ministry of Culture's Institute of Restoration, based in Tashkent, was to revitalise the historic centres of old towns by restoring, reconstructing or upgrading the monuments. Each monument had to be given a functional role that was appropriate to its architectural image. This was accomplished by researching and studying the original form and role of each: architects, historians and art historians took part in this exercise. Many, though not all, were from Bukhara.

There are 997 historical monuments in the immediate Bukhara region, and 500 within the walls of Bukhara town. These include twenty-four *madrasas*, forty-eight mosques, fourteen caravanserais, nine mausoleums, eight archaeological sites, four trading domes, three working *hammams* (and many more that do not), 265 listed old houses, and thirty-five varia that include the Ark Citadel, canals, and large sections of the city walls and its gates. The old town spreads over an area of roughly 3 by 2 kilometres, but the majority of the monuments are concentrated in the centre. As the buildings were still standing, the details of each brief varied accordingly. All had to be restored and provided with basic utilities. They had to look architecturally 'correct' in style; no new additions were permitted, although toilets and bathrooms were allowed. Most had lost their original

function; new functions had to be found for each, in order for this to be a living city.

The buildings have been restored to their original forms, using traditional decorative features and motifs. Enough was preserved of each monument and its decorative treatment (glazed tiles, paintings and carved bricks) to provide a basis for the rest of the reconstruction.

Many architects have worked on the town's monuments. Each project is planned, budgeted and implemented by the architects in Bukhara, but the design details are always worked out by architects sent from Tashkent; they have to approve the plan and the budget. The labour force is local, the specialised craftsmen or *ustas* usually belonging to a family with a long history in that craft.

Contractors, engineers and other specialists are supplied by the Ministry of Culture in Tashkent. The Municipality (*Hukumiyat*) of Bukhara is involved in the infrastructure, roads, communications, gardens and landscaping of the town; it uses its own personnel and budget. Foreign consultants are rarely used; an exception was made for studying the salt problem in Bukhara.

The old town functions well. It is used continuously by the people who live in the immediate vicinity as well as by the more general population. People walk around, shop – there is a variety of goods available, everything from basic groceries to antiquities – go in and out of museums and craft ateliers, have coffee in one of the coffee-houses, eat in a restaurant or at a shashlik stand, or sit quietly under the shady trees around the Labi Hauz pool. Sunday bazaars

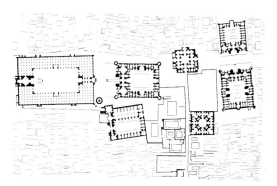

Reconstruction plan for the centre of Bukhara based on the seventeenth-century city layout

draw a crowd of thousands – one literally cannot walk in the streets for the sheer mass of humanity and the number of shashlik stands which belch clouds of smoke into the air. However, considering the number of people who use it on a daily basis, the old town is fairly well maintained and clean.

Nothing quite matches the magic of walking down a street in Bukhara and looking at the mass of its buildings and monuments. Indeed, the articulation of spaces in the old town has been much improved by the removal of 1950s-style Soviet buildings that had been constructed there; the few eyesores that remain are due to be pulled down soon. The old town of Bukhara now has a harmonious quality and appearance that is appropriate to its importance in the history of the development of Islamic architecture.

The restoration of Bukhara has had an incredible effect on the lives of its inhabitants. The upgrading of the old town, and the installation of such modern utilities as electricity, water and sewage, paved roads and pavements, have improved the physical conditions for all those who live and work within its boundaries. It has also brought economic security to the town by providing jobs and shops. Old Bukhara has been transformed from a derelict slum into a viable, functioning living space that is beneficial to itself and to the new town, into which is has been incorporated. It has given an aesthetic and cultural focus to the new town, and its monuments attract many foreign visitors who use the facilities provided by both and bring in badly needed hard currency. Old Bukhara has been saved and given a new lease of life.

That an important historic town of this magnitude is being restored by the local government is an incredibly important statement and contribution in an age when the destruction of anything old seems fair game, especially if it makes way for the new. In this project, the old town has been rehabilitated to play an active role in the new one, adding extra dimensions to both.

Shops in the old town are run by private individuals, signifying that the private sector has become actively involved in the project. At a time when money is tight and the financial outlook limited, the shops are all occupied – this was not the case three years ago.

The integration of the fabric of the old town into that of the new also seems to be working well. The urban flow of traffic and the interaction between the two has been carefully thought out, and it functions.

The project has changed in an important way from Soviet times to the present. Under the USSR, specialists were sent from Moscow and dictated methods and techniques to the local staff who could not refuse to carry them out; now, Bukhara and Tashkent work by consensus. The people of Bukhara are more involved. They appear to have a greater sense of identification with their own cultural heritage; more dedication to and combined awareness of its unique qualities; and, therefore, a stronger commitment to preserving it. There are also more technical staff employed by the project despite decreased funding and tighter budgets. The people of Bukhara are revitalising their city, not just for tourists, but for themselves.

In Soviet times, the restored buildings stood empty, they had no function and were seen only by the tourists on brief visits. Old Bukhara was dead. Now it is alive and bustling, its monuments functioning either in their original roles or in the new ones they have been given to play.

The credit for this must go to the Institute of Restoration, its members, the staff in Bukhara, and the Municipality. This is a collective work of a truly committed and dedicated group of people, with the support and involvement of the local community. Their achievement was recognised by the Aga Khan Award for Architecture in 1995.

REVITALISING THE CITY CENTRE

Preserving the architectural heritage and providing decent housing are not enough to make livable cities. A vital, bustling city centre, with a vibrant and growing economic base is essential. This is not achieved by turning a blind eye to the needs of the poor and the informal sector, or to the need for limits to real estate speculation in an historic area. The case studies presented here illustrate four methods of addressing these issues in four different cities. The Hafsia quarter in Tunis, Tunisia; Citra Niaga in Samarinda, Indonesia; Asilah in Morocco; and Lublin in Poland have all involved their citizens in the commercial transformation of their city centres, as well as the upgrading of their housing and neighbourhoods.

RENEWAL OF THE HAFSIA QUARTER
TUNIS, TUNISIA

Rawia Fadel and Ismaïl Serageldin

The medina – or old city – of Tunis is a major part of the heritage of the region and the world. Covering about 270 hectares, with some 100,000 inhabitants, it was added to the World Heritage List in 1981, for its great influence on the development of architecture and the decorative arts in the eastern Maghreb.

The Hafsia quarter of the old city of Tunis has deteriorated rapidly since the beginning of this century, due to the departure of its more affluent inhabitants for the new European-style city adjacent to it. World War II caused great destruction and there was further demolition in order to implement grand schemes to widen the avenues of the new city and build large apartment blocks.

The first phase of reconstruction, which sought to restore the traditional architectural and urban character of the Hafsia quarter, was completed in 1977 and received an Aga Khan Award in 1983.

The second phase of the project represents a broader effort to promote the renewal of the socio-economic base of the medina around Hafsia, while maintaining the traditional urban fabric where it exists and recreating it where it

has been destroyed. This phase of the renewal was launched as a component of the Third Urban Project co-financed by the World Bank and the Tunisian Government. It involved the rehabilitation of six hundred housing units and the construction of four hundred housing units, commercial and office spaces, and service facilities, largely by the private sector. The infrastructure of a 13.5-hectare area was also upgraded. The scheme has largely succeeded – and produced replicable measures – contributing to important institutional changes with far-reaching implications.

Physical constraints played an important part in the formulation of the project. Working with the Municipality of Tunis, and involving the Agence de Réhabilitation et Rénovation Urbaine (ARRU), the Association pour la Sauvegarde de la Médina (ASM) prepared a detailed master plan for the entire project site based on a number of key surveys.

Physical and socio-economic surveys carried out at an early stage determined user requirements and the type and extent of interventions needed in terms of rehabilitation, or demolition and construction. They evaluated whether

Plan of Hafsia showing phases I (light grey) and II (dark grey)

The new infill and the restored buildings integrate well into the old medina of Tunis

Many houses are provided with open spaces such as balconies, internal courtyards or gardens

construction work could be carried out while the units were occupied and what financial arrangements were required in relation to the ownership status of the occupants. The surveys also identified the number of additional housing units needed to relocate some families in order to reduce overcrowding, or to provide temporary accommodation for those whose units could not be rehabilitated while they remained in them. Thirty-five families later refused to leave the temporary housing units. Those tenants, or de facto occupants originally ineligible for loans from the National Housing Savings Fund, gained a new status, becoming owner-occupiers in newly constructed housing areas on the western edge of the city. This sensitive relocation plan for the involuntary resettlement – confirmed by an ex-post survey conducted by Harvard University in 1994 – is a major effort in an area many authorities have given no attention, and where success has been rare.

The ASM also undertook another survey of the physical conditions and characteristics of each building and piece of vacant land. Accordingly, a site plan was prepared which identified areas and buildings targeted for rehabilitation, reconstruction or demolition. Detailed studies, designs and construction drawings were carried out for buildings requiring restoration or rehabilitation. Designs and complete construction documents were produced for vacant land and for areas requiring infill or demolition and reconstruction. This included housing units, office and commercial spaces, and social service facilities.

Detailed studies were also carried out for the infrastructure. Particular attention was paid to the planning of improvements required to the network of roads and pedestrian paths in order to meet the needs for access, for communal outdoor spaces, and for proper storm drainage, while also ensuring minimal impact on the traditional urban fabric.

An architectural vocabulary based mainly on the traditional architecture of the area was developed and has been successfully used. Characteristic features of this include plain white walls; large projecting or recessed wall blocks for the articulation of the facade; the skilful use of contrast between white walls and deep openings and dark windows; arcades and arched openings for building entrances and entrances to alleys to articulate urban spaces; traditional bay windows and patterns of ironwork for window grills and balcony rails; light wood canopies above windows and balconies; and the development of decorative features and traditional motifs for the treatment of external wall corners and the wide decorated frames around main entrances.

The road network between the buildings is very narrow and confined to allow separation of vehicular and pedestrian movement. Outdoor landscaped areas are infrequent. However, the design of most housing units has provided internal courts or secluded balconies. These spaces allow families to create their own private landscaped areas.

Work to upgrade, install and construct utilities, infrastructure networks and facilities has been as carefully implemented and as far reaching as the architectural programme. It consists mainly of the following:
— providing water and sewage networks with connections to each plot or building;
— installing and connecting gas, electricity and telephone service facilities and networks to all buildings, with provision for connections to future buildings on vacant lots;
— resurfacing the internal road network with pavement cobblestones;
— providing proper slope and storm drainage connections;
— installing outdoor lighting in all streets with standard permanent lighting fixtures mounted on the exterior walls of buildings, as well as on vacant sites and buildings under construction where temporary fixtures are installed on posts until it is possible to replace them with standard wall-hung fixtures;
— providing facilities for solid waste collection and disposal, including containers placed on a number of selected sites and special collection carts suitable for narrow streets;
— providing social service facilities, including a nursery, a clinic and a public bath.

The technology, materials, labour force and professionals used to carry out the work were essentially local, differing little from those commonly used in Tunis. Most of the work did not require specialised skills, with the exception of restoration. The project provided on-the-job training for national professionals involved in the restoration, rehabilitation and reconstruction of historic areas, and the management of urban development. Apart from the contributions of a few foreign architects and economists during the first phase between 1970 and 1973, and the involvement of the World Bank in issues related to finance, the Hafsia II project was carried out by Tunisian professionals, in close collaboration with the private sector and with the involvement of the local community.

The financial plan included arrangements to make it possible for property owners to secure finance for rehabilitation work. Recent changes in the rent freeze law, which allow property owners to raise the rents of rehabilitated units based on improvement costs, should make it more attractive for property owners to borrow for rehabilitation.

An important feature of the financial plan was the institution of a cross-subsidy system which was developed following a study of the socio-economic characteristics of the area's inhabitants. Under this system, older houses are exempted from contributing to the costs of up-grading the streets and the infrastructure, and a special rehabilitation fund is created from revenues generated by selling building plots and property in the medina (in addition to funds received from the World Bank). The arrangement has been successful financially and has generated more funds than expected. Indeed, when the ex-post financial evaluation of the project was done, it showed a net profit of over a million dollars after the cross-subsidy.

The Hafsia project has been instrumental in the formulation of effective financial arrangements to achieve social objectives. The residents have been encouraged to own and rehabilitate their housing units through arrangements made with the National Savings Fund for Housing (NSFH). The NSFH had previously been lending only for buying land and for new construction. Changes in the policies of NSFH allowed lending for the upgrading and purchase of existing buildings. Following upgrading of the infrastructure, land and property values went up. Several

vacant plots were then sold to private developers at profit. The proceeds were used to support the housing fund which provided subsidised loans to the needy. The project has succeeded in enabling the inhabitants to rehabilitate and own their units; ownership has reached about 80 per cent.

The project addressed the requirements of households with different socio-economic characteristics. This included assessing when past residents of Hafsia who opted to rehabilitate their homes with or without loans needed to be relocated in temporary houses during the process, as well as answering the needs of potential new residents.

Minimum housing standards were established: for the very poor they specified a separate housing unit containing two rooms, a bathroom and a small kitchen, or the equivalent of about 40 square metres per household. The monthly rent was established at 18 per cent of the household income. For households which opt and qualify to buy, the ceiling for the monthly payment was established at about 22 per cent of the household income. About 134 households have been affected by the new construction and demolition programme. Of these, forty-six families qualified to own housing units in Hafsia as their monthly incomes exceeded 150 dinars. About twenty-three families with monthly incomes of less than 120 dinars could be rehoused in rental units in Hafsia. The remaining sixty-five families had to be rehoused, in affordable new housing, outside the Hafsia quarter.

The rehabilitation component targeted about 60 per cent of all the housing units in the Hafsia quarter (about six hundred housing units). It is now over 90 per cent complete, and the target is expected to be fully achieved within two years.

The work undertaken in Hafsia has succeeded in mending and restoring the traditional urban fabric – the street network, the common areas, and the harmonious relationship between the building blocks in terms of their form, height, mass, colour and detailing. The urban design takes advantage of the existing layout and city elements (for example, the bridge houses) to provide a variety of vistas, an interesting degree of complexity, and a reasonable degree of differentiation and identity.

As a result of this, the image of the quarter has changed: it is no longer viewed as a socially undesirable area, but as one sought after by families from various socio-economic groups for its cultural and aesthetic qualities, as well as for its convenient location and services.

In 1994, Harvard University analysed the impact of the Hafsia project based on a socio-economic survey. The main findings indicated that the overall social impact of the project was positive, even though it was not possible to rehouse in Hafsia all of the original residents. The overall economic impact was also positive, as the investment will be fully recovered before the due date. The quarter has become very attractive commercially, and residential buildings have begun to include more commercial activities than anticipated. The commercial vitality, however, is putting pressure on residential uses. Property auctioning to private developers was economically successful and property values increased greatly. Most developers changed the houses they built into garment factories (which provide employment, even for workers from outside Hafsia).

The tremendous success of the Hafsia Project resulted in a second Aga Khan Award for Architecture in 1995. Noting that it had not only empowered the local residents, but had also dealt sensitively with those who had to be displaced, the jury praised it:

For having successfully revived the socio-economic basis of the old medina, while remaining committed to respecting its unique scale and texture. The Hafsia district is once more a vibrant locus of economic and social intercourse. Institutional success, community involvement, financial and economic viability, an excellent public–private partnership and a sensitive resettlement programme for the displaced, make this a success worthy of widespread study.

In some houses the upper storeys bridge the street below

The narrow streets have shops at ground level and housing above

The new buildings have adopted the traditional architectural vocabulary

REHABILITATION OF OLD ASILAH
ASILAH, MOROCCO

Ismaïl Serageldin

Asilah is a city of history and culture. It is a rare case where the drive for the renewal of the city and its economic base was promoted by intellectuals relying on culture, rather than by businessmen relying on commerce.

The origins of the town go back to Phoenician times – the city was then called Zili. In later medieval times, it became a Portuguese trading post and the defensive walls built in that period are still extant. Nowadays, the town of Asilah is at once a harbour, a market, a centre for cultural events and a summer resort. Its architectural heritage has been revived on the initiative of a group of intellectuals including the Vice Mayor and Minister for Cultural Affairs, Mohammed Benaïssa, and the painters Mohammed Melehi and F Belkahia. The rehabilitation process has been going on for twenty years and consists of restoration work on various buildings as well as general improvements to the infrastructure.

Asilah is situated on the Atlantic Ocean on the north-western tip of Morocco, 45 kilometres south-east of Tangiers. The total population exceeds twenty thousand, but the historic core – which was restored – has an estimated population of 3,500 and covers 9 hectares.

It was at the initiative of Benaïssa and a few of his friends that the process of renewal began. The first part of the rehabilitation process concentrated on painting, paving and restoring some of the most visible parts of the medina – work which involved both artists and the local population. The second created a special cultural festival that made Asilah a destination for many intellectuals from all over the world, and which was so successful that it grew to a *musim*, or season.

The organisation of the first cultural *musim* in July/August 1978 provided the opportunity for the Ministry of Culture to restore a section of the city ramparts and to refurbish the large and luxurious Raissouni Palace (an early twentieth-century structure). This building was transformed into a 'palace of culture' and includes art studios and a hall reserved for cultural gatherings. An open-air theatre was set up in the old part of the city, within the Portuguese walls, and an area for film shows and permanent exhibitions of plastic arts was also provided. Within the constraints of a limited budget, the *musim* succeeded in attracting artists from various countries.

Further rehabilitation work continued and consisted principally of:

Location plan showing the old medina of Asilah

The integration of existing and new buildings along the seafront

— the restoration and rehabilitation of historical buildings such as the Portuguese fortifications and the al-Kamra Tower;

— the construction of new houses within the medina, built to replace dilapidated structures;

— the rearrangement of public spaces for commercial activities – such as the market place at the foot of the fortifications and the introduction of decorative pavings and murals designed by local artists (for example, the Place Senghor);

— the continuous maintenance of individual houses, public buildings and mosques;

— the improvement and extension of the infrastructure, including running water and sewerage systems and pavements.

The newly built private houses within the medina occupy irregular plots left by the partial or total demolition of older structures. Often, these new houses integrate elements salvaged from the ruins, such as doorways and arcades. The construction work has been conducted by local *muallims*, or master masons, and workers using traditional construction techniques and materials; the labour was also entirely local.

It is rare to see a local community take charge so completely as it did in Asilah. Even more important is that what was started by the élite quickly became a movement involving everyone. Such local level action is a different manifestation of empowerment, and an important one. It received an Aga Khan Award in 1989.

(Based on information provided by the Aga Khan Award for Architecture's library and documentation services.)

Paving of the streets made a noticeable difference and encouraged owners to renovate their houses

Crenellations and cornices provide a unifying element in the distinctive architecture of Asilah

CITRA NIAGA URBAN DEVELOPMENT
SAMARINDA, INDONESIA

Ismaïl Serageldin

Since so much of the real commercial activity that accompanies urban growth tends to be informal, it is surprising that commercial urban development schemes aimed at renewing city centres almost invariably displace the poor, and destroy the informal traders and street hawkers; the bulldozers move in, all in the name of progress. Thus it is encouraging to look at a scheme that did not displace the poor but made them partners in its design and implementation.

The 'Citra Niaga' is an innovative urban re-development programme begun in 1983, the result of a close collaboration between local and central government bodies, and between the private sector and the local community. The project transformed a former slum area into a planned urban and commercial complex, achieving a balance between formal shopping arcades and informal open-air market stalls, with the participation of the street hawkers.

Citra Niaga is located in the centre of Samarinda, the provincial capital of East Kalimantan. The site was inhabited by a low-income, migrant population working in the informal sector. It was a dilapidated and unhygienic section of the city.

The project was executed in phases. In addition to cleaning up the area, it provided 141 shops arranged in arcades and seventy-nine smaller shops to cater for high- and medium-income groups; twenty-four stalls, provided free-of-charge for street vendors and hawkers from the low-income bracket; and public amenities including infrastructural and recreational facilities.

The shopping arcades and market stalls are set in landscaped spaces with pedestrian precincts. Vehicular traffic is restricted to the periphery of the complex.

The variety of commercial activities provide animation while, at the same time, generating resources to subsidise the open market stalls. The layout of public spaces, equipped with simple and practical amenities like a covered podium for public entertainment, has made the complex more than a shopping area: it has become a real centre, a social gathering place where different income groups intermingle. The architectural content is simple but functional – using traditional roof forms to create a homogenous relationship between the different components of the complex.

The street hawkers now have stalls integrated into the overall development

The overall design shows a good mix of traditional and contemporary features

Citra Niaga is highly regarded as a national pilot project, particularly for its work to integrate stalls for the street hawkers and vendors who are usually overlooked. The project is also an example of the manner in which public–private co-operation can take place. But above all, it is the scheme's ability to empower the marginalised that makes it remarkable. Citra Niaga received an Aga Khan Award for Architecture in 1989.

(Based on information provided by the Aga Khan Award for Architecture's library and documentation services.)

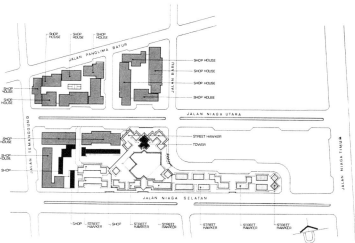

Spaces between shops allow for pedestrian interaction and rest

Site plan showing the inviting project layout which allows each group an appropriate location

PARTICIPATORY PLANNING PROCESS IN LUBLIN, *POLAND*

Mona Serageldin, Boguslaw Trondowski and Sameh Wahba
in collaboration with Ewa Kipta

To my surprise, the work of enabling people to create the space they occupy has proven to have a more significant effect on that space and the relations between residents than direct design.
(Ewa Kipta)

In 1990, the urban planning unit of the City of Lublin initiated a participatory planning process to upgrade and rehabilitate older districts by engaging residents in the development of their neighbourhoods. Dwindling central transfers and tight budgets necessitated the mobilisation of community resources to improve the urban environment. Strong backing from the city government was necessary to begin this initiative. The reform-minded city president was willing to experiment with innovative ideas and the City Council endorsed the rehabilitation of existing buildings as a component of Lublin's overall housing strategy.

Prior to 1990, urban regeneration in Poland relied on demolishing older districts and replacing them with housing estates. In Lublin, however, lack of resources prevented implementation of most urban renewal plans. Areas slated for demolition experienced progressive deterioration and disinvestment. Distrust and apathy deepened among frustrated and discouraged residents. Planners and architects did not perceive the resourcefulness of the people who struggled to retain livable conditions in their dilapidated dwellings. They also failed to grasp the limited extent of outside investment needed to make significant improvements.

This may seem surprising in a country where preservation of the historical and cultural legacy is a national policy, and where stringent conservation practices safeguard the fabric of the built environment as well as individual buildings and require restoration to archeological standards. Indeed, the first proponents of rehabilitation were creative professionals who, because of previous work experience in historic districts, understood the process of incremental transformation by successive generations of residents. This ability to visualise the cumulative impacts of small changes by a multitude of participants lies at the core of successful enabling strategies.

The Lublin initiative was launched in two lower income districts, Bronowice and

An unimproved building in Kosminek

A partially restored building in Bronowice with a micro-enterprise on the ground floor

Kosminek. Bronowice has a population of four thousand and encompasses an area of 80 hectares, thirty of which are residential. The population of Kosminek is approximately two thousand. The fabric of both districts consists of a nineteenth-century core of multi-family housing (originally designed for workers employed in adjacent factories), a zone of good quality single-family housing, and more recent unserviced extensions consisting of illegally built housing on small plots carved out of former fields. The illegal structures did not conflict with the older fabric and could be easily integrated into the neighbourhood development plan.

A precondition for resident involvement was the removal of the threat of building condemnation. Furthermore, to dispel widespread apprehension among residents, regularisation had to avoid disruption and minimise regulatory controls. Demolition was limited to structurally unsound buildings and dimensional regulations were limited to height and bulk.

Because the districts were designated as urban renewal sites thirty years earlier, residents had been denied access to infrastructure. They could not even connect to existing networks, on the grounds that all existing housing was 'temporary' pending demolition. Repairs to buildings were also prohibited except for major roof leaks. The resulting pent-up resentment and distrust of municipal authorities was a major obstacle that had to be overcome by the local initiative team.

Regaining the residents' trust required a long process of listening and learning when and how to intervene. Based on a shared vision of the future, this process has been a cutting-edge concept in Poland, for both the professionals and the citizens involved. Moreover, architects and city planners had to discard their conventional roles as sole shapers of the built environment and sole arbiters of appropriateness concerning development standards and aesthetics. This reassessment did not come easily in a situation where the architects' education and practice reinforced the application and enforcement of technocratic norms.

Lublin's community-planning process has required an extensive and sustained outreach effort over the past two years. The plans for both Bronowice and Kosminek were approved by the City Council in December 1993. This approval has regularised the status of unauthorised buildings. Residents now feel secure from both displacement and challenges to their occupancy rights. The Act for Support of Local Investment, passed in January 1994, commits the City to support the upgrading process through public/private sharing of infrastructure costs. Residents along each street designate representatives who negotiate with the City regarding the necessary improvements and sign the cost-sharing agreements. The City's share is modulated to reflect the economic situation of residents and the physical conditions of the site. Taking into

A new building in Kosminek with a micro-enterprise on the ground floor

Rehabilitated house with an added second floor and a new unit at the back

consideration the cost of house connections borne by residents, the City is covering approximately 50 per cent of the total investment.

In September 1994, the City decided to institutionalise the local initiatives programme as a key environmental improvement strategy. To accomplish this goal, the Unit for Housing and Urbanisation at Harvard University Graduate School of Design is providing Lublin with technical assistance and training funded by USAID. The institutional framework structures an interface between the City and the community to foster participation, partnership and empowerment. At the community level, neighbourhood development committees were established to bring a broader perspective to bear on the concerns and activities of street representatives. Within the City two interlinked, working groups were established: the Programme Team with part-time members drawn from the staff of different departments to take on the critical role of catalyst and enabler; and the Co-ordination Group including the heads of the City's strategic departments to provide the technical and political support. The Programme Team, headed by Ewa Kipta, was formalised in January 1995, and the Co-ordination Group was established as a standing committee for city development in February.

The local initiatives team has maintained an ongoing dialogue with residents to set priorities for upgrading activities and leverage, and to co-ordinate public and private inputs in the development process. To stimulate housing renovation and expansion, it has expedited permitting procedures and changed zoning regulations to foster the development of home-based income-generating activities and micro-enterprises. It has inventoried potential sites for the development of business incubators and contacted organisations providing support services to small businesses in order to help local micro-entrepreneurs access these resources. The team raised awareness of environmental issues and prompted residents to contract private services for solid waste collection in areas that city-operated vehicles couldn't reach due to narrow and unpaved roads. They also managed to mobilise residents to participate in the cleanup and landscaping of the river front by the Lublin

Foundation for Environmental protection. Lastly, it is engaging residents in the improvement of public space. Seemingly small gestures such as repairing a pavement or planting and maintaining a tree have already made an impact on the quality of the urban environment and contributed to a new image for the neighbourhoods.

Participatory planning and sustained citizen involvement have achieved results exceeding initial expectations. In two years, 137 houses have been renovated and fifty new buildings have been constructed. Only six shops existed in the neighbourhoods before the programme was initiated. Today, fifty-five shops have been opened in the rehabilitated buildings and eighteen buildings have been entirely converted to commercial use. Close to 120 people are working in these micro-enterprises. In addition to the inputs of residents themselves, ongoing construction activities are providing work for over one hundred people engaged in the building trades.

Lublin's local initiatives programme was selected from six hundred submissions worldwide as one of twelve Best Practices to receive an award for excellence in improving the living environment at the Habitat II conference. It was the only winner from Eastern Europe and the CIS region. The programme has amply demonstrated that participatory planning and community-based development processes adapted to the dynamics of the local economy can ensure the sustainability of revitalisation efforts, despite diminished public inputs. By building in a strategic component in partnership initiatives, the programme makes significant contributions to the livability and economic vitality of the city's diverse neighbourhoods. The architect's involvement in guiding this process, despite the fact that it did not centre on direct design contributions, has proved invaluable. As an advocate for a coherent urbanity the architect/planner in an enabling role allows the actions of individual homeowners to be informed by a broader community agenda.

Drawing the residents into the planning process allows them to claim the eventual changes as their own . . . Creating the awareness of a need for a quality environment seems to be the most rewarding part of my role. (Ewa Kipta)

REACHING THE POOREST: THE RURAL WORLD

The majority of the poor still live in the rural world and will continue to do so for the next generation. Finding a way to reach them has challenged the imaginations of architects from Hassan Fathy to ADAUA. But probably the most successful solution has been found and implemented by the economist Muhammad Yunus in Bangladesh. He founded the Grameen Bank and devised an effective system of micro-credit for the landless poor. The success of the enterprise shows that even the most insurmountable obstacles can yield to determination. It is a testimonial to what confidence in the empowerment of the weak and the marginalised can achieve. In an area where most government programmes have failed and few NGOs have succeeded in expanding the scale of their operations, Grameen is a signal success deserving recognition and praise.

THE GRAMEEN BANK HOUSING PROGRAMME
BANGLADESH, INDIA

James Steele and Ismaïl Serageldin

Bangladesh is a poor and populous land of 120 million inhabitants, the vast majority of whom can be considered rural. Of those, over 50 per cent can be classified as landless. In a country where the national income per capita is estimated at about US$275 per annum, the income level of the landless rural population is virtually that of the destitute. It is they who are hit hardest by the annual monsoon flooding and the cyclones; their suffering only exacerbated by the fact that they usually have to live on marginal lands, in frail, feeble shelters or makeshift homes that leave them exposed to every risk. They are locked into a cycle of poverty and destitution.

The Grameen Bank Programme was started in 1976 in the village of Jobra by Muhammad Yunus, the then Director of the Rural Economics Programme of the Department of Economics in Chittagong University. It set out to provide credit to the rural, landless poor for income-generating activities, and offered it to them at the low interest rate of 16 per cent. Because they lack the collateral, the poor are normally barred from obtaining credit from official institutions. They are then forced to borrow from local lenders at exorbitant interest rates.

The significant and truly revolutionary aspect of the Grameen Bank Programme was that it required no collateral from its poor customers. They had to repay their debt through their own commercial or artisanal activities. The condition of the Grameen Bank Programme was that people organise themselves into small solidarity groups to act in concert and with discipline. The group would oversee the punctual payments of the loan instalments of all its members – if these were missed, the group had to pay. This ensured that solidarity helped overcome the vulnerability of individual members and, where needed, provided sufficient peer pressure from within.

Loans are given to individual members or to the group as a whole with each loan being valid for one year only. It is paid back in weekly instalments, each being 2 per cent of the total amount. In addition, every group member deposits 2 taka per week (TK40 = US$1) as a personal saving which is placed into the group fund account. When a group member receives a loan an obligatory deduction of 5 per cent of the loan amount, known as group tax, is deposited into the group fund account where it can be used for the benefit of the members. On approval from

Each basic house is built on a rammed earth base, has bamboo and jute walls, and a corrugated iron roof

Borrowers are responsible for the design of their homes, having satisfied the basic requirements of the Grameen Bank

the group, members can borrow from this fund: these funds are also refundable to the members after ten years with interest. In addition, a member pays a weekly sum into an emergency fund which is set at a rate of one-fourth of the total interest being paid to the Bank. This is basically an insurance against default, death, disability, accident or other disasters. The maximum individual loan is TK5,000 (US$166), although proven borrowers can get more. The smallest loan on record was for TK1.

The Grameen Bank Programme was transformed into an independent bank with the name of the Grameen Bank in 1983. The Government provided 60 per cent of the initial paid up share capital while 40 per cent was held by the borrowers of the Bank. Successive reductions of the government share have resulted in the government holding less than 10 per cent today, with the remaining shares belonging to the borrowers. This represents a signal achievement in terms of institutional independence and steps towards full financial autonomy.

The Bank's conditions for membership are as follows: any person whose family owns less than 0.5 acres of cultivable land, and whose assets together do not exceed the market value of one acre of medium quality land in the area, is eligible for loans for income-generating activities from the Grameen Bank. Only one person from each household is allowed to become a member. To get a loan, he or she must form a group of five like-minded people from similar economic and social backgrounds. Sometimes, several groups in a village get together and form a centre with an elected centre chief and deputy chief. The centre chief then conducts the weekly meetings and is responsible for the observance of the Bank's rules. Between two and ten groups can form a centre, the average being six. Ninety-three per cent of the Grameen Bank members are women. In fact, the belief of the Bank is that not only are women a potential and reliable economic force, they are also the prime agents of social change in the society and their well-being translates into the well-being of the entire family, much more so than the men. This is borne out in many field studies. Over the past decade, the members of the Bank have evolved

a manifesto called the 'Sixteen Decisions' which is adhered to by all the groups.

Each centre is looked after by a Grameen Bank branch assistant who attends the weekly meetings and collects the payments. These assistants identify future customers, distribute the loans, supervise the groups under their charge, and ensure that accounts are kept and payments paid back on time. In fact, they are involved in many extension activities with the groups. Each Grameen Bank branch assistant is responsible for up to ten centres and, with an average of six groups per centre, that means seeing up to three hundred people per week. The assistant works from a branch office which supervises and services some sixty centres located in around twenty villages. Ten branch offices are supervised by one area office covering an area of 200 square miles which in turn is supervised by a zonal office. Each zonal office looks after an average of eight area offices. These zonal offices have a high degree of autonomy and are given a free hand to administer their areas. The head office is based in Dhaka and oversees the whole project.

By June 1996, the Grameen Bank had over 2.1 million members spread out over 35,753 villages in fourteen zones of Bangladesh. There are 1,056 branches in operation looking after 61,547 centres. Of these centres, 57,577 consist of female groups and only 3,970 of male groups. Excluding the housing loans, the Grameen Bank has currently distributed just over TK59602.90 million. In June 1996, the recovery rate was an astonishing 98 per cent.

The Housing Loan Programme was limited in October 1984 after a National Workshop during which Grameen Bank workers exchanged their practical experiences and ideas. From this exchange it became clear that as the income generating capacity of the Grameen Bank borrowers improved, their demand for better housing increased. The decision was then made to start a Housing Loan Programme as a specific and important part of the Grameen Bank operations, and not just as an adjunct to another loan. Its aim was to make funds available for Grameen Bank members of good standing for building new houses or rehabilitating their old ones. Only members who regularly paid their dues on time and who adhered to the rules were considered for these loans. And because the sums involved were much larger than those that were available through the general loan programme, new lending policies and procedures had to be set up. Preference, as always, was given to the most needy.

A two-tier system was established. The larger loan, for amounts up to TK25,000, was called the standard housing loan, while the smaller loans of up to TK12,000 were called basic housing loans. The housing loan is charged at 8 per cent interest instead of the 20 per cent interest charged for the regular or short-term loans.

The Grameen Bank Housing Loan Programme covers a wide geographical zone which includes a range of architectural styles. Most of the houses occupied by the poor are single-storey with one or two rooms at the most, with the cooking area and animal shelter clustered around the house forming a yard or outdoor work area. The house space is multipurpose and acts as a sleeping area and a storage space for all the utensils that the family owns, including those for income generating activities such as weaving and sewing. A ceiling-level platform, built using the base of the roof truss, frequently acts as the repository for valuable objects. A number of the houses have interior altars.

The archetypal house form consists of a rectangular building with a pitched roof and hipped or gable ends. They are small and can measure from 2 by 3 metres to 4 by 7 metres in size. Most pre-Grameen Bank houses seem to have been smaller than those built with the loans. All are built on raised earth platforms to preserve them from the rising flood waters of the rainy season. Some houses have windows, others do not. Doorways, made of bamboo matting or wood, seem to provide most of the interior light and usually open inwards.

In the central area of Bangladesh the houses are mostly built with a bamboo or wood frame that can support a lightweight wall made of either bamboo matting or jute sticks. The facades are frequently plastered with mud. Thatched roofs are made of grass, rice stems, bamboo matting, or jute sticks. None of these materials are durable and they have to be replaced almost every two years. Yearly flooding adds to their brief lives. Therefore, thatched roofs are dispensed with as soon as the owner can afford to buy corrugated sheeting. Sometimes even the walls are replaced with sheeting.

The Grameen Bank Housing Programme proposes a basic house which can be built with a basic house loan and which can be modified and extended by the borrowers if their resources permit it. A standard house loan would, of course, provide a larger house but the materials remain the same. The basic house has a usable floor area of at least 20 square metres. Four reinforced concrete columns, manufactured by the Grameen Bank, are supplied to each borrower. The early Grameen Bank Housing Loan houses had wooden posts but these proved to be susceptible to termites and unstable during the floods. A more secure structure was needed.

Reinforced columns were introduced and have proved very successful. They provide a secure attachment point for the walls and also the roof (so secure that in times of flood people can sit on them). The columns are sunk upright into the ground at the four corners of the houses to a depth of 0.5 metres.

Additional posts, made of wood, bamboo or reinforced concrete have to be provided by the borrower and depend on the resources to hand. The loan allows for the purchase on the local open market of eighteen corrugated-iron sheets, each measuring 2.44 by 0.82 metres to cover the basic house with a simple pitched roof. This can be supported by a wooden or bamboo roof frame which, in turn, is supported by the four columns and any other secondary posts.

Walls can be filled with any material chosen and bought by the borrower who also decides on the number and types of windows and doors he or she requires. Grameen Bank staff favour doors and shutters that open inwards because they are not exposed to the sun and rain and therefore survive longer. Heights of plinths and floors are left up to the borrowers. The Grameen Bank has a plan for the basic house and makes sure that at least the minimum requirement is satisfied. However, the borrowers are basically responsible for the design of their houses. And even though they usually choose materials that

The single living space accommodates a kitchen area (sometimes outside under the overhang of the roof), storage and sleeping spaces

Quick drying mud is an important structural element, used both as a component of the bases and sometimes as a coating for the walls

belong within the local architectural style for their roofs and as fillers, no two houses seem the same.

Since mid-1988, the programme has also required the borrower to build a latrine for the house, using a latrine base with siphon and cement liners for the pit. These are manufactured by the Grameen Bank production yards and are provided with the rest of the materials at the start of work, but the Grameen Bank does not advise on their placement. The Grameen Bank does not involve itself with such details as the siting of a house, its orientation, or its relation to nearby buildings. Neither does it provide loans for public facilities, though some centres are using their savings fund for setting up schools for the younger children.

The reinforced-concrete pillars and the latrine kits are manufactured at thirty-four different sites across the country, using moulds which are easily transportable according to demand. The local branch office only needs to specify the amounts required. The masons running the production units receive a loan from the Grameen Bank at 16 per cent interest to help them finance the work. The borrower has to arrange the transport. Two pillars can be moved in one rickshaw van or three men can carry one pillar at a time. Each column is 3.35 metres long and 13.3 centimetres square in cross section. The production of these pillars operates as an independent income generating unit. A mason and five labourers can produce twenty-nine columns per day; each sells for TK380. They are made with a mix of two parts cement to four parts sand to two parts of brick chips. Each column also has fourteen 10-millimetre diameter bars and thirteen links. The person who takes out the loan pays the workers.

The concept and the design of the houses originated in Bangladesh. Many of the materials are local, although corrugated sheeting is essentially an imported product. Cement comes from local factories as well as from Indonesia, and the steel is milled in Bangladesh.

All the Grameen Bank Housing loans are given to the rural poor who live in rural settlements, or on plots of land sited by road embankments or fields. There is such a great variety in these houses that they cannot be described in general terms. The following descriptions of three specific loans demonstrate this.

Afiya Begum has been a member of the bank for nine years. She took out a house loan after her home was destroyed by floods. Her new house stands on a platform measuring 14 square metres, which rises several metres above the level of the paddy fields that surround it on three sides. The Dhaka–Tangail road runs along the fourth side. The house consists of a single room measuring 6 by 4 metres and an outbuilding of 2 by 4 metres that functions as a kitchen. The two sections are positioned at right angles to each other and so create a small open-air space that also acts as an outdoor cooking area.

An improvised shelf on the concrete corner post, a safe place for possessions

Corrugated iron forms a simple pitched roof supported on a bamboo and wood frame

Afiya Begum also intends to build an outside latrine on the site. Her husband and three children share the house. In this small space she keeps goats and ducks which help to augment her income. She bought the land from a local landowner with a loan from the Grameen Bank.

Kamala Begum lives with her husband in a new Grameen Bank loan house, situated some 50 metres away from the Dhaka–Tangail road, in a small compound with three other houses. Her husband owned the 850 square metres of land on which they built their house, but since she was the Grameen Bank member, the title deeds were transferred to her name. The houses have a large open area between them and sit high above the level of the paddy fields around them. Kamala Begum earns her living by sewing, using a machine she bought with a loan from the Grameen Bank. From her savings she bought her husband a rickshaw.

Rahissa Begum has a two-room, 5-by-3-metre house which was built with a Grameen Bank housing loan in the village of Habibpur, in the Munshiganj Upazila district. The village consists of many clusters leaving little room for expansion. Her house faces the river bank on one side and a small communal open area on the other three. She has a kitchen shelter. Her husband owned the land and it was transferred to her name. Although it is difficult to expand she wants another loan to add an extension for her four sons and one daughter who live with them.

Her income comes from two milk cows which she bought with Grameen Bank loans.

The Grameen Bank Housing Loan Programme started in October 1984 with a potential house loan of up to TK15,000. In 1984 a total of 317 loans were made. The number rose slowly, and then more after the disastrous floods of 1987, and by June 1996 there were 339,945 borrowers.

This increase coincided with the two-tier house loan system mentioned earlier. In 1988 these loan plans were modified and a new small housing loan was introduced for amounts up to TK8,000 and renamed the basic housing loan. The sum was later raised to TK12,000. The moderate housing loan was increased to TK25,000. The basic loan is taken seven times more often than the moderate. In all cases, it is not necessary to make the maximum amount. The basic house loan, which has to be repaid back at 5 per cent interest, breaks down as follows:

Reinforced concrete pillars at TK380 each	TK1,520
Two bundles of corrugated iron sheets	TK4,500
Sanitary latrine	TK500
Other materials, roof frame, etc	TK5,480
Total	TK12,000

By the end of June 1996, the Grameen Bank had distributed TK5,479.61 million to 340,000 borrowers, at an average of TK15,373 per head. Payments are made on a weekly basis at a minimum rate, but if the borrower wishes, the repayments

Workers prepare building materials

Many women undertake construction work for their homes

can be larger and the period shortened. Now the maximum limit is ten years.

But the maximum period is fixed in the ratio of years to thousands, so TK18,000 has to be repaid in eighteen years. The repayment rate is running close to 100 per cent.

The maintenance cost for these houses is very low. It basically includes the replacement, every two or three years, of the jute and bamboo matting on the walls. The reinforced concrete pillars should last for eighteen years maximum, although the corrugated-iron sheeting will not survive that long. Termite attacks and humidity cause the deterioration of the organic materials used in the walls and these have to be replaced at intervals.

Technically, these house loans are sound. The houses provide effective protection from the rain, an important point in a monsoon country, and for most households are a significant improvement on their traditional housing. They also withstand the floods better. After the 1988 floods, the Grameen Bank home owners spent less money repairing their houses than those who had traditional homes.

This was also apparently true for the disastrous cyclones that hit the Bangladesh coastline in the spring of 1991. The Grameen Bank house owners fared much better and they lost less of their belongings.

The level of technology required for building and maintaining these houses is perfectly adapted to the users. All the materials are familiar and no new technical innovation is required. The residents have faith in the materials used in their houses, all of which have been tried and proved successful. Innovative techniques and materials would probably not be popular with people of such modest needs.

The response to the programme has proved its success. The number of borrowers is increasing and the Grameen Bank hopes to add another US$2 million to their fund by 1992. The Grameen Bank also plans to expand the areas it serves, but only after it has trained the necessary staff to carry out this work. The staff are dedicated to the objectives of the Bank. In fact, they are really the ones who are responsible for the success of the operation and it could not have been achieved without their hard work.

The reaction of the users has been difficult to measure. The Bangladesh Institute of Development Studies has tried to assess the reaction of the Grameen Bank Housing Loan house occupiers. From a survey conducted in the Tangail, Dhaka and Rangpur Zones, on a sample of 116 cases, the benefits of moving into the new houses is given as follows in the order of their importance:

— possessions are saved from damage caused by rain;
— possessions are saved from thieves;
— decreased intensity of diseases;
— increase in the quality of work;
— increase in social dignity;
— capability of doing more as confidence grows.

The most significant factor seems to be that everyone who was visited had plans to go on adding to their houses. Many have already enlarged their original investments by adding better windows, cement floors, a roofed verandah, or even additional rooms. However, one cannot and should not disassociate the physical product of a house and the provision of a loan from the fact that Grameen Bank has been providing general loans for the promotion of finance-generating activities among the Grameen Bank borrowers. The housing loan and its end result is an effective and successful operation because the borrowers are already engaged in activities stimulated by a general Grameen Bank loan which enables them to cope with the repayments on the house and embellish it with savings made from their self-employment.

The two parallel aspects of loans offered by the Grameen Bank are what makes it successful. It would not be possible for poor people to take out a loan for a house without an income to repay the loan. The income-generating loans provide them with the means to do that. This is an extraordinary project which is a shining example of empowerment. It was recognised by an Aga Khan Award for Architecture in 1989.

REACHING THE POOREST: THE URBAN WORLD

The huge growth predicted for urban areas in the Third World presents many problems, and one of the biggest challenges lies in empowering the poorest members of these societies, hitherto marginalised, to have a constructive role in their own future. Since the cases are many and the issues complex, rather than presenting a selection of otherwise unrelated projects, this section concentrates on the urban scene in Pakistan. The Orangi Pilot Project Housing Programme in Karachi and the Khuda-Ki-Basti Incremental Development Scheme in Hyderabad are both inspired solutions to reach the homeless and to empower them to create real communities for the future.

THE URBAN SCENE IN PAKISTAN

Arif Hasan

Fifty-eight per cent of Pakistan's urban population lives in *katchi abadis* (squatter settlements) and informal settlements, un-serviced or under-serviced areas which are growing at a rate of over 10 per cent a year against a total urban growth of 4.8 per cent. Unemployment figures are also high by national standards. Households cannot function without earning women but there are few well-paid job opportunities for them. Most houses in the settlements are of poor quality and are semi-permanent.

However, there is a powerful informal sector in these settlements which develops them to an extent, providing jobs for almost half the employed, and giving credit for businesses; but services are substandard, to say the least, and the credit systems are exploitative.

Almost all settlements develop some form of community organisation to lobby for services in their area. Often residents come together to do development work themselves, mostly related to water supply and sanitation. However, almost all of this work is substandard and either falls into disuse after a short period of time or requires intensive maintenance which proves a financial burden to the community.

In the older settlements formal groups also exist. They are social welfare organisations registered with the Social Welfare Department from whom they receive a small sum of money. They operate mother and child clinics, and vocational and primary schools, and lobby incessantly with state agencies for services. Most of the services these formal groups provide are of very poor quality and function erratically.

In many settlements new leaders are emerging. They are young, educated, second-generation *katchi abadi* dwellers. The old clan-based leadership is fading away and most settlements now tend to be multi-ethnic and multi-caste.

Very few NGOs in Pakistan are directly involved in community development work in the urban sector and many of their programmes are 'donor driven'. Very few have tried to develop models that are replicable by government. Most of them try to provide health and education services, help communities to lobby the government, assist them in preparing proposals for acquiring funding from donors, or raise 'environmental concerns' to which the communities do not relate. In addition, they, and the CBOs they work with, do not have the technical or managerial capacity to absorb funds and most have to depend on external funding sources for their daily functioning. Research shows that CBO and NGO attempts at development fail because of lack of access to technical and managerial know-how. This failure discredits community activists and results in despondency in the community. (In addition to this, the structure of NGOs, and many CBOs, is patriarchal, and while their leaders provide people with facilities, they are reluctant to empower them as they fear loss of their own power.)

These problems are compounded by the fact that the NGOs are unable to get appropriately trained professionals to work with them. Most professionals are trained on the First World model and see services as something that have to be delivered; the concept of participation is alien to them and they have little or no knowledge of the dynamics of low-income communities and settlements. Yet, still only two academic institutions in Pakistan have changed their curriculums to make them relevant to the larger context of urban areas.

The government of Pakistan has a number of programmes to alleviate poverty. The most relevant of these has been the Katchi Abadi Improvement and Regularisation Programme (CAPRI), in operation since 1978. Though even this has been far from successful. Only 13.85 per cent of *katchi abadi* households have been regularised and only 22.41 per cent have been, or are in the process of being developed. At this rate it will take over eighty years to regularise the existing settlements. Meanwhile, *katchi abadis* continue to grow nine times faster than they are being regularised.

The government's commitment to participatory development is clearly stated in its last three five-year plans. The link between development, environment and community is also clearly spelt out, along with the decentralisation of planning and the implementation of development measures, and the importance of women in the process. However, as in the case of the NGOs, most government planners and technocrats are trained conventionally and have a poor understanding of the sociology and economics of poor urban communities, and of the process of change that has destroyed the old social economy.

Government and academic institutions in Pakistan are, by and large, engaged only in desk research, their aims and objectives notwithstanding. Almost all research at government and academic institutions is technical and scientific. Social research is seldom undertaken, and even when it is, it is purely academic in nature.

Most government institutions do not have the technical or managerial capacity to operate the conventional programmes they are saddled with, let alone the participatory ones they are being asked to run.

Yet, in spite of the constraints mentioned above, there have been successful community development projects in the NGO sector in Pakistan. The government is trying to integrate these models into its planning and implementation processes through a number of pilot projects. However, the attempts made so far have been frustrated since the pilot projects are not given the freedom to operate independently and are viewed with suspicion and hostility by powerful vested interests in government and politics. In addition, more time and effort is spent on putting these schemes together on paper and carrying out surveys of various types, than in involving the community in their planning and implementation. This often results in projects reverting back to function on conventional lines, or being abandoned altogether.

However, in recent years some NGO projects have expanded to an extent that the communities they serve are sufficiently organised to pressurise government agencies to link their work with community initiatives. Conversely, the government needs to relate its work to these NGO projects in infrastructure development, and health, education and credit programmes because without such linkages its own programmes simply cannot work. This interaction between government and NGO participatory development projects is forcing changes in government perception and planning at the local level. Participatory planning in practice is emerging at government level, more as a result of this interaction than any policy decision or setting up of pilot projects by the government. As architect Perween Rahman, director of the Research and Training Institute of the Orangi Pilot Project, says: 'Things can only work if governments participate in people's programmes and not if people are asked to participate in government programmes.'

It is against this setting that the successful efforts of the Orangi Pilot Project and the more recent Khuda-Ki-Basti scheme can be truly appreciated. They are living proof that the architecture of empowerment is possible and feasible, provided that the architects and planners change their attitude and learn to trust the people.

THE ORANGI PILOT PROJECT HOUSING PROGRAMME
KARACHI, PAKISTAN

Arif Hasan

The Orangi township lies in the west district of Karachi and consists mainly of *katchi abadis.* Covering about 8,000 square metres, it has a population of around one million living in 94,122 houses. Before the Orangi Pilot Project (OPP) began its work, the township had no sanitation system and almost no piped water supply facilities.

The OPP was established in 1980. It considers itself a research institution whose objective is to analyse the most pressing problems in Orangi, and to discover viable solutions. It does not carry out development work but promotes community organisations and co-operative action, and provides technical support to such initiatives. It consciously attempts to develop models that can be replicated by government and for this purpose it keeps its overheads, staff salaries and related costs at the same level as government institutions. In addition, it keeps detailed documentation of its work. The OPP feels that communities supported by expert professionals who understand the context within which they work, can support its objectives.

Based on these principles, the OPP operates programmes for low-cost sanitation, low-cost housing, health and family planning, education, supervised credit for small family enterprise units, and women's work centres. Three of these are well developed and are being replicated by various NGOs and the government sector in Pakistan (they are the Low Cost Sanitation Programme, the Health Programme, and the Credit Programme for Small Family Enterprise Units).

The Low Cost Sanitation Programme is the most developed of the OPP projects. It is based on the OPP motivating the residents of Orangi to organise themselves at 'lane level' to collect money and then to manage the construction of underground sewage systems in their lanes and neighbourhoods. The sewers drain into open *nalas* or natural drains. The OPP provides the lane organisations with plans, with estimates of the labour and materials required for building the system, and with construction tools. As the people finance and build the sewers themselves, they also maintain them. The average cost of the system for a sanitary latrine in the home, the sewer in the lane, and the collector drain, works out to about 900 rupees (US$30), which is affordable to the people.

A lane before the OPP helped the residents lay a sewage system

The same lane after the sewage system had been installed

Houses constructed without the help of the thallawala

It is now difficult to find a lane in Orangi which does not have an underground sanitation system: 5,517 lanes out of 6,230 have an underground sewage line; and 82,574 houses out of 94,122 now have sanitary latrines. The people of Orangi have invested Rs63,795,297 (US$1.72 million) in this effort. If this work had been done by the local government it would have cost at least the equivalent of US$12 million. The OPP's administrative, research and extension cost for this effort works out at Rs3,428,588 (US$92,664).

The OPP sanitation programme has shown that there are four levels of sanitation: the sanitary latrines in the house, the sewer in the lane, the collector drain, and the trunk sewers and treatment plants. The first three levels are called 'internal development' by the OPP and the trunks and treatment plant are called 'external development'. The Orangi experience has shown that an organised and technically supported community can finance and manage the construction of internal development provided external development can be provided by the government if a natural disposal point for sewage does not exist. The same internal–external divide exists for water supply. It is this concept that the OPP has promoted with state agencies and NGOs and CBOs since 1983.

The Health Programme focuses on mothers. Initially, mobile teams delivered advice to them. As a result, 90 per cent of children were immunised and over 45 per cent of families adopted birth control. However, this approach still failed to reach over three thousand families, and a change of method became necessary. Today, the Health Programme undertakes a training function and anchors the programme institutionally in schools, private clinics and family enterprise units. Those trained in this manner regularly hold mothers' meetings and deliver the OPP advice package.

The impact of the health and sanitation programmes has been remarkable. Infant mortality has decreased from 130 per 1,000 in 1982 to 37 in 1991, and infant morbidity during the same period has fallen from 18.94 to 8.29.

A more equitable relationship has been established between the Orangi community organisations and the local government as a result of which the community will be able to access local government funds and resources more easily. It has been noticed by the OPP that as soon as a lane has built its sanitation system residents start improving their homes. Real estate prices in the lanes where sewage systems have been established increase immediately by 15 to 20 per cent. There is more social cohesion now and the regular quarrels that once took place between women and households regarding filth in the lanes are a thing of the past. It has also been reported that a number of girls for whom no marriage proposals were forthcoming have now got married as they live in better surroundings.

The programme has been so successful that it is now being replicated by the Sindh Katchi Abadi Authority (SKAA) in forty-nine settlements in Karachi and by NGOs in seven other cities in Pakistan. To make this possible the OPP acts as a consultant to the SKAA, the Karachi Municipal Corporation (KMC) and the relevant NGOs, and training is given at the Research and Training Institute (RTI) at the OPP. Orangi Township serves as the demonstration area.

In 1982, members of the communities who had worked with the OPP on the sanitation programme requested its assistance in improving their houses. The OPP observed that by 1982 over seventy thousand housing units had been developed in Orangi without any assistance from the government. Most of these houses were poorly designed and constructed but it was obvious that a process for their construction was in place. The OPP felt this should be fully understood before a new housing programme was developed. As a result, a research study was carried out. This was undertaken by students from the Department of Architecture and Planning at the Dawood College of Engineering and Technology (DCET), Karachi. It was completed in 1983. The study aimed to understand the sociology, economics and technology of housing in Orangi.

Its first finding was that 93 per cent of houses in Orangi were built with the financial and technical assistance of the local building component manufacturing yards operated by entrepreneurs. These yards exist in all neighbourhoods. They are known as *thallas* and their owners as *thallawalas.* The *thallawala* provides materials on credit to house builders – and sometimes cash credit as well – materials which he delivers to the site. He also helps in the design of the house; he takes on part contracts for building the house, or, alternatively, he supplies masons to the house builder who wishes to do the unskilled work himself.

Regarding the materials and designs used in building, the DCET survey found that – again – 93 per cent of houses were constructed from concrete blocks. Roofs were initially galvanised iron sheets, which were replaced over the years by asbestos sheets. These in turn were often replaced by reinforced concrete slabs with the intention of raising a first floor. It was noted that the foundations and walls could seldom carry the concrete slabs safely: walls cracking and the plinth settling as a result. Additional design defects which were identified consisted of poor utilisation of space, and poor ventilation and lighting, the importance of which did not seem to be understood.

It also became clear that in addition to bad materials, bad workmanship by poorly trained masons was responsible for building defects; the better trained masons work in the more affluent areas of the city. The masons and other skilled labour working with the *thallawala* needed technical advice on the right mix of concrete, curing, proper sizing of supports for galvanised iron and asbestos sheets, correct overlaps and slopes to the roof, and water proofing walls at the plinth level. This was not available to them.

The socio-economic reasons for the defects were also identified, and can be summarised as:
— bad relationships between the owner and the mason during construction;
— the disproportionately high hire fee charged by the *thalla* for the construction tools;
— most people hire a mason for construction and act as unskilled labour themselves;
— both the builder and the owner accept that as the house is that of a poor man, substandard construction and materials are normal;
— the unequal relationship between the *thalla* and the owner.

The OPP could not find an alternative to the *thalla*: its housing programme would have to work with existing *thallas* and improve them, or consider establishing its own. It was important to reduce the cost and improve the quality of the concrete block, and to provide better roofing materials. An extension project was required to inform people of the OPP findings so that they could establish a more equal relationship with the *thallas*, and better supervise their building.

Credit remained a problem. The OPP was in no position to operate a loan programme for housing, and did not want to interfere in the informal system of land acquisition, development and delivery which seemed to function to the satisfaction of the communities (and which also had powerful vested interests).

Houses constructed with the help of the thallawala

Common defects in houses made with the assistance of the thallawala

Common defects in houses made with the assistance of the thallawala

Thus, the OPP decided to support the existing system by improving technology and creating more equitable relationships between those involved.

It decided not to operate a *thalla*, but instead came to an agreement with Raza Sahib, a *thalla-wala*, whereby it would work with him to develop new materials and techniques of construction.

A programme for training masons in the use of the new technologies was also initiated at the *thalla* and people were advised to use these masons for the construction, extension and improvement of their homes.

All this took time. The R&D for the housing programme began in 1984 and, with brief periods of inactivity, was reasonably developed by 1987. The housing package developed by the OPP consists of the following:
— appropriately designed in-situ concrete foundations for a two-floor construction along with the loan of steel shuttering to cast them;
— 150-millimetre machine-made load-bearing concrete blocks and 100-millimetre non-load-bearing partition walls;
— precast concrete batten-and-tile roofing with a maximum span of 4.90 metres and a most economical span of 3.65 metres;
— precast concrete staircases;
— trained masons and design advice.
The OPP recognised that it would be impossible to reach every house builder and mason in a population of one million. To redress this it has published instruction leaflets focusing on critical issues which it has supplied to house builders and masons either individually or through the *thallas* that have adopted the OPP programme.

Many masons, even though they have been trained by the programme, advise their clients to build reinforced concrete roofs rather than precast batten-and-tile roofs. This is because the profit margin of a mason is much larger when he builds an in-situ reinforced concrete roof and a framed structure. To overcome this, an agreement between some *thallas* and masons has been worked out whereby the masons get a commission from the *thalla* if his client uses the batten-and-tile roof.

After Raza Sahib's *thalla* was developed with OPP assistance, three other *thallas* applied for assistance. This consisted of giving credit and advice for introducing the technology developed at Raza Sahib's *thalla*. The credit given to each *thalla* works out at an average of Rs71,250 (US$1,925). Since then an additional forty-six *thallas* have benefited from the technology.

There has been an extraordinary increase in the production of concrete blocks due to this mechanisation; the Orangi *thallas* have become a major supplier of concrete blocks, battens and tiles to the construction industry in Karachi. Almost 60 per cent of the blocks manufactured in Orangi are exported to other localities of Karachi. This demand was not foreseen when introducing the programme.

The OPP introduced mechanisation at the thallas *to produce blocks*

The OPP introduced precast battens and tiles at the thallas *– these moulds were made in Orangi*

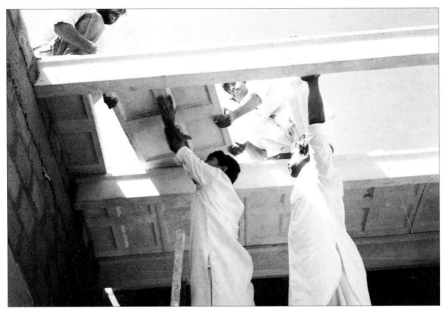

Placing the precast concrete which will be capable of supporting a floor

The thallawala *at work*

This industry has generated a large number of jobs for Orangi residents. While a proper survey on this has not yet been undertaken, new jobs clearly relate to transportation, loading and unloading; and there has been an increase of over 100 per cent in the number of workers employed at the *thallas*. These workers have also experienced an increase of about 30 per cent in their earnings. This is due not only to an increase in wages, but also to the fact that labourers can work every day as opposed to the fifteen to twenty days per month previously. It has been estimated by the OPP that production at the four *thallas* which it supports has gone up by over 300 per cent and the income of the *thallawala* by over 100 per cent.

As a result of the housing programme all new construction in Orangi now uses machine-made concrete blocks which are not only stronger but larger, and hence easier to use and quicker to build with. Much of the new construction also uses the batten-and-tile roof and the foundation, ventilation and other technical details developed by the OPP. This has not only improved the housing stock but has also increased its value by 15 to 20 per cent.

However, there are a number of issues that need to be addressed if the programme is to be even more successful. One of these is quality assurance for the building materials, another is whether to give advice to those who do not use the new materials, and, if so, how to do so outside the current framework. There is also the issue of scale: the OPP is unable to cover all the needs of the huge Orangi community and a replicating mechanism is needed. Above all, there is the question of sustainability.

The programme can be sustained if it becomes self-financing and resolves the other issues. The OPP explored the possibility of financing a group of young architects/technicians to set up a self-supporting design and supervision office in Orangi. The likelihood of this office succeeding is strong as the Orangi squatter settlements are in the process of being regularised, and for regularisation the residents require a plan of their existing property which the office can prepare. In addition to which, straight after regularisation, residents start extending and improving their homes.

This design and advisory practice consists of two young people. They were given a three-month course in the OPP's low-cost technology, including planning, estimating, designing, surveying and supervising. Originally they worked from the OPP office but they have now moved to premises in a part of the Orangi settlement to which they belong. They are receiving clients and are being paid for their work. In addition, the World Bank Shelter Project in Karachi has asked them to provide technical assistance to the houses in Orangi for which the Shelter Project is providing credit. They are also to monitor the construction of these houses.

Many important lessons have been learnt from the project. It has demonstrated that technical and financial support to the informal sector can improve the way it functions to such an extent that it can serve the formal sector as well. The OPP has also shown that by making relationships more equitable in an existing informal housing process, housing quality can be improved and a far larger number of households can be reached than through conventional programmes for housing credit and materials. Its work with the *thallas* shows that sophisticated technologies can be simplified to an extent that they can be used by small entrepreneurs to develop and market affordable components for low-income communities. Finally, it recognised that the major problem for informal-sector, low-income communities is that they do not receive expert professional advice. It also acknowledged that conventionally trained professionals cannot give this advice because they have little or no knowledge of the processes that are producing housing in the informal settlements. By devising a project for students from professional academic institutions to participate in this informal process, the OPP has enabled them to contribute to its betterment in the future. It is they who are becoming the practitioners of the architecture of empowerment.

KHUDA-KI-BASTI INCREMENTAL DEVELOPMENT SCHEME
HYDERABAD, PAKISTAN

Lailun Ekram

The 5,550-acre Gulshan-e-Shahbaz housing scheme is located on the highway connecting Karachi and Hyderabad. It is 12 kilometres south-west of Hyderabad city. The scheme is based on a grid layout of fifty-two sectors, which has not worked well. Many of the plots remain vacant and, apart from the model homes built by the Hyderabad Development Authority (HDA) and the site office, the entire area is barren. All the homes, built in barrack style, are unoccupied; and the barrack layout is visually regimental and unappealing.

In an attempt to change this situation and to reach the poorest, the HDA decided to experiment with a new approach in four of the fifty-two sectors. This project, called Khuda-Ki-Basti (which means 'Allah's Settlement'), is based on the idea that people should settle before houses and infrastructure are built; and that, once settled, they can develop their housing and the infrastructure incrementally, as and when they have the resources. The Incremental Development Scheme in Hyderabad imitates the approach followed by the illegal subdivider; it is characterised by ease of entry, immediate delivery of the plot, and incremental development of the houses and the infrastructure. By formalising this approach, the scheme empowers a group that ranks among the most vulnerable in Pakistan.

The challenge was greatest in trying to reach the homeless among the poor, those who spend most of their lives without access to any permanent shelter. This required making land and credit available to people who had no hope of getting either through formal channels.

The scheme operates a reception area for new arrivals. Screening applicants by their stay in the reception area helps establish their suitability for the scheme, and is one of the key-points in the determination of plot allotment. Technical assistance was provided in the formulation of housing standards to stimulate and promote the input of the users, and to explain building techniques for self-help in construction. Supervision and maintenance of the housing were also provided.

A co-operative system was used to manage utilities, including decisions of access, building management, revenue and maintenance.

A support group (NGO) was established to assist the scheme with technical, educational and moral support to make its work sustainable.

View of Khuda-ki-Basti

View of Khuda-ki-Basti

Settlement takes root as the brick-walled one-storey pucca *house replaces the* jhuggi *house of reed and wood*

The courtyard of the pucca *provides space and shade for domestic work*

Occasionally part of the dwelling is set aside for enterprise, such as this weaver's workshop

Plants make houses more homely and add to the sense of an established neighbourhood

The result of these efforts was the creation of a real community from those who were once poor and marginalised. In 1989/90, the population of Khuda-Ki-Basti was between twenty thousand and twenty-five thousand, with an average family size of 7.24 and an average household income of Rs1,567.

The success of the scheme owed much to the fact that it was able to reach the very poor without being hijacked by the middle-income groups. The sequencing of the design concept was also instrumental and innovative.

The key to ensuring that the programme remains focused on the poorest is the screening procedure. This works by a family arriving and staying in the reception camp for fifteen days. After screening by the HDA and down payment of Rs1,000, the family is then allotted a plot. Within fourteen days they must begin to construct their house otherwise the allotment can be cancelled. They design and construct the house themselves (a portion or complete) in any manner suitable/affordable with whatever building material or style they prefer. They may continue to improve, extend and beautify their homes. They also contribute, with the rest of the community, to all the main service lines within the site and all the primary roads.

While the householders are free to build as they choose, the first stage of their building usually takes the form of a *jhuggi* – a shelter where walls and roof are made of reed, wood, cardboard, or whatever gives protection and privacy from weather and people. From this stage the householders will incrementally build a one-storey, brick-walled *pucca* house.

The house-form always includes a boundary wall and a gate, and all plots are aligned with boundary walls on the road front. The incrementally developed house usually has two rooms, one verandah, one kitchen, a bathroom, a latrine and an open-to-sky courtyard. During the daytime, the courtyard is a multi-purpose work area for women and children (especially girls) and at night time it is the sleeping area for men.

Rooms have few small windows, and natural light within rooms is inadequate. Furniture is scarce, but all families have *charpayah* (rope matted beds). Some households have been allotted the adjacent plot, which they can use for farming (poultry and breeding livestock). Sometimes, a house is also used to accommodate small cottage industries, especially carpet weaving and embroidery, which are specialities of this region. Plots along the 18- to 40-metre roads now have a commercial function and are occupied by shops.

Today, 85 per cent of the plots have permanent houses made of brick or cement block, with cement-mortar pointed walls and reinforced cement roofs. The majority of these *pucca* houses are single-storey, only about 10 per cent are two storeyed. Facades are brightly coloured and have cantilever verandahs with jalley-work

Typical sector plan

Khuda-Ki-Basti emerges as a rooted community

railings. Construction work on these houses was undertaken by the owner, with technical assistance from SAIBAN (an NGO established in 1991), especially in foundation design.

After shelter came the utilities. The sequencing and participation of the community was ensured through the co-operative framework established by the monthly payment made by each of the households. Residents apply for individual house connection to all utility services after completing all required formalities and paying departmental charges. The residents qualify for procurement of utility services after payment of monthly instalments to the HDA against their total payment schedule.

Large 1,525-millimetre-diameter RCC pipes are laid under the streets for sewage lines. For every four houses there is one septic tank, which is joined to the two pumping stations. The water is recycled and used for the cultivation of adjacent land. Sewage lines within the houses are cast iron pipes.

Seventy per cent of the houses have individual water-supply connections. Houses without a water-supply connection collect household water from conveniently located pipes. The HDA is responsible for water supply and mainline distribution. The Utility WAPDA is responsible for the electricity supply and distribution.

A few houses have telephone lines. Facsimile and STD phone service is available commercially. Local and satellite television and cassette players are a favourite form of family entertainment.

The waste disposal system is still problematic. A community participatory system is being evolved as the solution.

This amazing project has been able to fulfil its objective of plot allotment through the adapted land tenure process. It has allowed the poorest section of the urban community to settle in a planned area with decent living standards. Their aspirations for a better life are clear to see in their house forms and their effort and enthusiasm to procure the infrastructure, stage by stage, through community decision and investment.

In each block of the sector, a community leader is chosen by the residents to lead them in decisions on infrastructure and maintenance, and to instill unity and motivation. These leaders liaise with the HDA, SAIBAN and other authorities.

As the house moves from the *jhuggi* shelter to the *pucca* house, the essence of permanency prevails. Here, ownership is pride: a sense of right and responsibility has become inherent in this community.

The driving force behind this bold project was the Director General of the HDA, Tasneem A Siddiqui, assisted by Mohammad Azhar Khan, the director of the planning and design section of the HDA, who was in constant contact with the users and helped solve their day-to-day problems. The NGO SAIBAN is committed to the welfare and growth within the township, under the leadership of Shahid Hossain, who is on site to organise, motivate and stimulate positive growth in Khuda-Ki-Basti.

This public–private co-operation is part of the success of the scheme. But more importantly, those involved have learned the lessons of Orangi; they have trusted the people, put them in charge, and empowered them to take charge. Like the Orangi Pilot Project, credit and income-generation played a pivotal role and the adoption of the people–land–housing–services sequence made it possible for the poorest to develop a thriving community.

The success of Khuda-Ki-Basti has stimulated and generated interest in many professional groups. It received an Aga Khan Award for Architecture in 1995.

UPGRADING THE SLUMS AND DENSIFICATION

Urban poverty is so extreme in many parts of the developing world that it challenges our very conception of human decency. However, the World Bank estimates that with proper policies to empower the poor and encourage community action, focusing on basic services rather than the highest standards (such as latrines rather than individual flush toilets), conditions can be transformed by an application of only 0.2 to 0.5 per cent of GNP over fifteen years. This is an infinitesimal amount in order to reduce infant mortality from waterborne diseases and to provide the dignity that comes from having access to basic facilities. Three projects clearly demonstrate the benefits which sensitive schemes based on community involvement can bring: the East Wahdat Upgrading Programme in Amman, the Kampung Improvement Programme in Jakarta, and the Home Densification Programme in Lima.

EAST WAHDAT UPGRADING PROGRAMME
AMMAN, JORDAN

Ismaïl Serageldin

By 1980, it was estimated that about 25 per cent of the greater Amman population lived in uncontrolled housing and settlements, where insecurity of tenure, overcrowding, limited infrastructure and poor housing conditions prevailed.

The East Wahdat Upgrading Programme was undertaken within this context. Its main objective was to upgrade some of the capital's squatter areas by introducing infrastructure and community facilities, and by legalising land tenure. The project was jointly financed by the World Bank, the Jordanian Government and the Jordan Housing Bank.

In a remarkably sensitive exercise, the Urban Development Department convinced the Amman Municipality to work with the poor; rather than raze the shanty town, they empowered the people to transform it. The Urban Development Department first conducted surveys to gather socio-economic data. Special regulations were then drawn up to allow a reduction in plot sizes and more flexible construction rules. The price paid by the residents for each plot included the cost of all infrastructural facilities as well as that of land. Credit was advanced to the poor. During construction, the occupants were not evicted.

With the help of neighbours, they moved their existing shanty structures to a corner of the plot as a temporary shelter. The first room of the new house was then built on the vacant space. The residents moved in, pulling down the original shanty and completing the rest of the house at their own pace.

The result is a thriving community with plots of varying sizes (ranging from 60 to 200 square metres) according to the needs and means of each of the 523 families. All plots are provided with water, sewerage, electricity and road access. Schools, clinics, community and vocational training centres were built and technical assistance was made available to the families to help them to build their own houses as well as fifty-eight shops and twenty-four workshops.

This project has succeeded in transforming a shanty area into a serviced urban community where residents no longer live in fear of eviction, but legally own the land on which their houses are built. Income-generating activities, such as vocational training, and commercial facilities and bazaars to sell handicrafts have also been introduced. The East Wahdat Programme received an Aga Khan Award for Architecture in 1992.

Site plan of East Wahdat

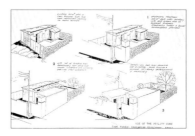

The process of upgrading existing dwellings through the provision of a utility core

Clean surfaced walkways replace the muddy walkways between houses

Ramshackle sheds in East Wahdat before the upgrading programme

The upgrading begins to transform the neighbourhood

Concrete frame buildings in East Wahdat after the upgrading programme

THE KAMPUNG IMPROVEMENT PROGRAMME
JAKARTA, INDONESIA

Ismaïl Serageldin

The provision of basic infrastructure and municipal services to the urban poor is of fundamental importance in upgrading slums, and in Indonesia it has been achieved with remarkable success.

The Kampung Improvement Programmes (KIP) began in Jakarta in 1969. Far from utopian in scope, early KIP initiatives concentrated on providing kampung residents in the capital with basic amenities – water distribution, drainage and access paving – which they could not organise and build by themselves.

Over the years the KIP has reached more than fifteen million low-income urban residents. In projects funded by the World Bank, the average cost varied from US$23 to US$118 per person (in 1993). Along with physical improvements on 11,331 hectares, KIP activities have also spurred kampung dwellers to invest in upgrading their housing and surroundings. Community spirit is fostered by the residents taking part in the construction and relocation and, in many instances, the community is involved in maintaining the roads, drains, water supply, sanitation facilities, schools and clinics that the KIP has brought to the worst neighbourhoods of Indonesia's cities.

By delivering basic services to the poorest and to areas of deepest environmental blight, KIP has set realistic goals and reached them. By stressing community participation, it has contributed to the growth of self-sufficiency and the spread of co-operation within poor neighbourhoods. By ensuring steady support of the KIP, the Indonesian Government (with World Bank help) has created a model which it has proved possible to replicate throughout the country.

The key to this model remains the proper definition of roles. The public sector does only what it has to to create an enabling environment – not least of which is the security that comes from titling of land to the poor – and to empower the poor to deal with their own environments.

The KIP's programme in Jakarta was the first such project to win an Aga Khan Award for Architecture in 1980. The KIP received two more awards for its programmes in Surabaya and in Yogyakarta (this is treated as a separate case study in this book).

(Based on extracts from the World Bank's booklet Livable Cities for the 21st Century, *1996.)*

High density and irregularly patterned kampungs pose a challenge to planners

The government had to provide the basic infrastructure

The people provided most of the labour to improve their environment

DENSIFICATION OF EXISTING URBAN FABRIC, *LIMA, PERU*

Mona Serageldin, Boguslaw Trondowski and Sameh Wahba
in collaboration with Gustavo Riofrío

To this day, I do not understand why people think of empty spaces when thinking of the city. Cities and houses already exist and little space is left vacant . . . We need to create in order to adopt, remodel, improve and enhance the quality of life. (Gustavo Riofrío)

A new settlement trend has emerged in Lima, Peru's capital, over the past decade. As the city's spread reaches its limit for feasible commuting distance, Lima's sprawling landscape of one-storey shanty towns is densifying through vertical expansion. Access to land is rightly regarded as the critical factor in managing urban growth. Peru addressed this issue in 1961 by institutionalising the regularisation of informal settlements and the release of unserviced land as the cornerstone of an urban development strategy. Public officials thought that this programme would be sufficient to solve the housing problem. Twenty years later wasteful sprawl, costly and difficult to service, is taxing municipal resources and testing the resilience of city dwellers. Overwhelmed government agencies have tended to equate enabling strategies with letting people solve their problems as best as they can on their own. This approach has become untenable in a situation where 70 per cent of the working poor have incomes below the poverty line. Young families have a choice to either live in the already overcrowded, but at least partially serviced areas, or to build in districts ever more removed from urban facilities and infrastructure. Their plight is fuelling spontaneous densification of regularised settlements and low-density *barriadas*.

To accommodate the rapid growth of the population, sustainable improvement strategies have to rely on reworking the existing fabric and utilising the skills, energy, and resources of the local communities. This is precisely the approach taken by urban planner Gustavo Riofrío working for DESCO, a Peruvian NGO. With support from the French city of Rezé and Programme Solidarité Habitat, he developed the Home Densification Programme to address the densification trend and its consequences through community participation supported by adequate technical assistance. Additions often constitute a safety hazard to the inhabitants since most homeowners rely on their own skills for both design and construction. Even those self-builders who can afford contractors prefer to retain the services of skilled

House prior to densification

House with second floor added

Quality brickwork produced by self-builders

craftsmen rather than professional designers. Unfortunately many civic groups and NGOs reinforce this attitude. *Their approach, which states that people build better than technicians, recognises that technicians do not understand people's specific needs, but denies the fact that people are not technicians.'*

In the past, where professionals have attempted to get involved in informal settlements, they have been met only with distrust. The densification programme started by Riofrío is changing this attitude by redefining technical assistance, setting up an instrument to finance housing additions, and establishing an institutional framework for managing the densification process. All three components of the initiative had to be developed simultaneously in order to guarantee the sustainability and replicability of the effort. The only subsidy provided covers the cost of the technical assistance needed to improve the quality of the additions.

The Home Densification Programme grew out of a realisation that spontaneous densification had severe shortcomings, endangering residents and degrading the urban environment. The programme focuses on the half-built houses as well as their setting – the underdeveloped neighbourhoods – as well as providing technical assistance to individual homeowners, who retain the power to make final decisions. This has helped to legitimise the programme. In order to overcome the deeply ingrained mistrust of outside experts the project had to demonstrate its commitment to local concerns and priorities. Special efforts were made to change building patterns that unnecessarily add to construction costs, to utilise building materials provided by local suppliers, and to train master builders living in the settlement.

The financing mechanism created relies on local resources. Capital from a local private bank is mobilised by means of a loan guarantee and is used to offer small loans at prevailing market rates. In a typical transaction a loan guarantee of US$100 and a grant of US$60 for technical assistance mobilise a private sector loan to the amount of US$400, thereby achieving a respectable leverage ratio.

DESCO is working with people in order to help them valorise their existing assets. Houses originally built as one-family homes, now have to accommodate multi-family dwellings and micro-enterprises. This requires refashioning existing space as well as expanding the structure. Professional input is needed to address basic issues of ventilation, illumination and circulation as well as more difficult issues of cooperation among neighbours, such as the sharing of staircases necessary to reach safely the upper floors. The cornerstone of the process is the community's involvement in the improvement of its living environment. *'Because we work in an occupied space, it is imperative to do so with those who have individually and collectively produced that space.'*

The pilot project in one of Lima's southern districts, the Villa El Salvador, has achieved outstanding results: 201 households have designed extensions and improvements; 137 families have improved their houses; 11 households have built new units; 6 families rented accommodations erected through vertical expansion; and 31 micro-enterprises were established in remodelled premises. The pilot has demonstrated the potential of empowering 'self-builders'. *'Our task as an NGO is to show the feasibility of an enabling strategy. For the future, our commitment is to work with people in replicating and scaling up the process.'* Consequently, the densification initiative is currently undergoing a transition from pilot to programme. The ultimate goal is to replicate the model across cities nationwide.

Architects and planners cannot work in isolation. Dialogue and consensus building underlie successful neighbourhood improvement strategies, particularly when self-reliance is an objective of the community-based improvement process. *'The architect's task lies in matching different views on how a neighbourhood ought to develop without killing the deep meaning of each approach to create tenable compromises.'* The Home Densification Programme manages to reclaim for architecture its social component. *'. . . we need to create a new city with the existing structures and existing people . . .'*

BUILDING NEW SETTLEMENTS

Not all urbanism involves upgrading existing settlements. New settlements are sometimes purposely built. The case against the grandiose schemes of new utopian cities has usually rested on the absence of a sound economic base. Presented here are two schemes that demonstrate – to varying extents – how this problem can be resolved by devising effective processes of growth and participation. New Shushtar in Iran was built for the workers of a nearby plant. In this case the architect's sensitivity compensated somewhat for the less than full involvement of the community in the design. The Ismailia development project in Egypt, however, was based on full empowerment of the community and resulted in a major rethinking of the country's urban policy.

SHUSHTAR NEW TOWN
SHUSHTAR, IRAN

Ismaïl Serageldin

In 1973, the Karoun Agro-Industries Corporation decided to build a satellite town to house the employees of a sugar cane processing factory nearby. This was to provide individual housing as well as communal facilities and infrastructural services. Development of Shushtar New Town was also intended to revitalise the old town and to accommodate expansion generated by industrial growth in the region. Shushtar New Town, in the Khuzistan Province in south-west Iran, is across the river from the old city.

Kamran Diba of DAZ Architects, Planners and Engineers was the driving force behind the new development. He was sensitive to the architectural tradition of the area, knowing that the residents wanted to retain some of its characteristics.

Old Shushtar is one of the oldest fortress cities in Iran. It was an island city on the Karoun River during the Sassanian era when it also became the winter capital. The fortress walls were destroyed at the end of the Safavid era from AD1502 to AD1722.

The local architecture is most influenced by the Safavid era. Buildings are constructed from mud brick and have evolved into a formal arrangement of four rooms separated by the cross-formed barrel-vaulted *iwans*, the central intersection being an open courtyard.

In the desert climate, it was found that a dome over the central courtyard produced a pleasant cooling effect. The roofed patio, *tanabi*, became a place of general assembly. Consequently, the courtyard was moved to one side of the house. Depending on the climatic conditions (which vary north and south), the direction of access into the house, and the occupant's wealth, two courtyards were built – one on the hottest side and one on the coolest. The courtyard on the street side was usually lower than street level. This facilitated the flow of rainwater into a central pond in the patio that stored water for drinking and irrigation.

The car and other modern innovations brought some changes to the town. New roads, connecting the main gates and passing through the city neighbourhoods, were built at the cost of old bazaars, caravanserais and public baths. All new buildings are constructed of materials such as steel, concrete and kiln-fired bricks.

The design of New Shushtar follows the pattern of traditional Iranian architecture which is introverted, taking its forms from climatic

Pattern of courtyards and parapet crenellations give a modern echo to traditional architecture

The individual homes are havens of privacy with lush interior courtyards

Shaded narrow streets are flanked by superb brickwork

constraints, available local technology, and the country's culture. The massing of the buildings is a parallel arrangement of mostly one- and two-storey houses which are clustered along narrow streets following traditional models for privacy. The treeless narrow streets are paved with brick. The top floor of the houses is built along the street front to maximise shading. Most residential streets are oriented east–west so that houses catch the prevailing north wind. To further foster privacy and neighbourhood activity, traffic is prohibited in the residential areas.

Public buildings are grouped along the east–west pedestrian boulevard, and are designed to give neighbourhood identity to each block in the traditional manner. The town is planned on a grid but, to punctuate the dense residential fabric, public buildings are set at an angle to the grid. In the residential clusters, each of the 650 units use the traditional organisation with multi-functional rooms arranged around a courtyard and roof terraces for sleeping. Most rooms in the two to four room houses are 5 metres by 5 metres; smaller ones are 3 metres by 3 metres, or 4 metres by 4 metres. Thick walls, small windows and street entry through a small protected space are also traditional features. Parapet walls surrounding the roof provide shade.

Although this is not a case where the future residents were involved, the sensitivity of the architect helped. Residents were satisfied with the houses and the layout of the dwellings. They felt comfortable with the designs, which cut down excessive heat and sunlight, and the layout and natural lighting which follow local customs and architectural tradition.

The project is also faithful to the traditional architecture of the region in creating an urban environment which encourages social interaction. By the design of its spaces, it generates a communal sense. The contrast between the vast public spaces and the dense fabric of the streets and residential neighbourhoods also offers visual and spatial diversity. As does the topography and slight slope of the ground which afford changing perspectives as the street and surrounding buildings step up towards the town centre. The attractive decorative brickwork grilles beneath the windows, and on the roof parapets and the entry arcades also provide ventilation. Mosaic tiles mark entries to the houses and embellish street signs.

Construction of the new town started in 1976, and most of the first stage was completed by 1978. This stage was planned to function as an autonomous unit and to accommodate about four thousand inhabitants. Political unrest in 1979 disrupted the work. During the hiatus in construction, squatters and refugees moved into the complex and then took over the site. But the excellence of the design appealed to the people who had moved in and to the new government authorities. Implementation of the remaining phases continued.

Shushtar New Town is relevant to the cultural values of Iran and maintains a continuity with the past. Its example of urban housing is unique as a large-scale new town conceived and produced by local designers and builders attempting to satisfy indigenous lifestyles and contemporary goals of industrial development. Their work was genuinely adopted by the people, even though they had not participated in its initiation.

ISMAILIA DEVELOPMENT PROJECT
ISMAILIA, EGYPT

Ismaïl Serageldin

At a time when the Egyptian Government was still trying to deal with the problem of massive urban growth by building new towns in the desert – public housing which invariably proves too expensive and too small – the Ismailia Governorate's development projects, launched with the help of Culpin Planning, put the emphasis on upgrading existing settlements and on community self-help construction.

As early as 1974, the Ismailia master plan argued for an alternative to the conventional public-sector social-housing programme, which although intended for the poor could only be afforded by 10 per cent of the population. An alternative use of the public subsidy was proposed to produce more social housing for the lowest income range. It would also encourage home ownership which had hitherto been beyond the reach of all but the highest income families. An education programme was designed to train local administrators to implement the policies. Development was to be self-generative with gradual improvement of the service infrastructure, using income from land sales. The approach was to be tested in two key areas of Ismailia, a city on the Suez Canal, about 135 kilometres from Cairo.

Hai el-Salaam is a northern extension of the city that had grown uncontrollably. Abu Atwa, formerly an agricultural settlement, is about four kilometres south of Ismailia. Both sites were planned and surveyed focusing on plot rationalisation. Existing settlers were given legal rights of occupation, frequently with adjusted plot boundaries. There were emergency relocations – though these were kept to a minimum by thoughtful design – in cases where existing houses stood on sites reserved for roads or public purposes. Their owners were given priority in the allocation of new plots. Public housing was provided for those who could not afford to build their own. Rules for the allocation of new plots were drawn up and the plots surveyed, demarcated and offered for sale.

About 80 per cent of the Hai el-Salaam houses were individual homes built on plots averaging 100 square metres. In 'informal' areas they are predominantly single-storey, mud brick or rammed earth. In 'formal' areas they are baked brick, often with a reinforced concrete frame, allowing for future upward extension. In Abu Atwa, construction mostly followed a traditional village style using rammed earth.

The key to the success of the project is the empowering of the local community

Government support was needed for streets and infrastructure

The buildings, inhabited even unfinished, continue to grow vertically and horizontally

The shanties become cities; stability, tenure and empowerment allow the poor to have structures similar to those of the middle class

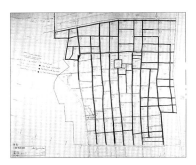

Plot rationalisation was crucial in setting the configuration of the site plan

The inhabitants' demands were simple. Security of tenure was the highest priority, followed by piped water, roads and sewerage. Lack of security prohibited individual investment in buildings. To upgrade areas, it was vital not to force out the population. In the new development, a mix of income groups was accommodated, giving low income groups at least their proportional share.

Planning is based on a hierarchical arrangement of streets and avenues with a main centre and neighbourhood sub-centres. Shopping needs are met primarily by shops on housing plots, in addition to a central market. Other centralised facilities include schools, community centres, a clinic and a post office. Following the traditional Islamic pattern, neighbourhoods tend to be defined by local mosques. Streets in the existing areas of each settlement were upgraded and adjusted to improve circulation and services.

There are many advantages in combining the upgrading of an existing settlement with the creation of a new development in close proximity. The latter provides space to accommodate families relocated from the original town, and space to build new social and community facilities to serve both communities. Utility networks can service the old and the new areas.

The Project Agency provides different house plans for families who can not afford to pay for professional assistance. Houses may be self-built or contracted to builders in the project.

Constructing the Hai el-Salaam extension of the city of Ismailia in 1978 represented a critical departure in the development of low-income housing in Egypt. It was one of a handful of areas where this new approach was applied. It channelled public housing subsidies towards broadened local initiatives. For the first time in Egypt, physical and institutional guidelines for housing were established primarily to respond to the poor. In 1980, Abu Atwa began exploring the same strategy.

The Government donation of land was the largest single subsidy. A grant of 100,000 Sterling pounds from the British Government provided the initial capital. Later, revenue to the agency amounted to almost 3,500,000 Egyptian pounds. This has been used for infrastructure and low-income loans because small-scale credit proved essential for the success of the scheme. Within ten years, ninety thousand people had been housed in Hai el-Salaam and Abu Atwa. They had achieved the security of titled ownership.

Hai el-Salaam and Abu Atwa housing is controlled by local and personal decisions. The project empowered thousands of families to utilise their collective imagination, energy, time and funds in order to create their own habitat. It was a pioneering effort and has influenced national housing policy elsewhere in Egypt. It was recognised with an Aga Khan Award for Architecture in 1986.

CREATING COMMUNITIES

Can design help the creation of the social bonds that constitute a real community? Can the process of building and upgrading help communities come together? Three cases show that it can. The most purposeful effort is that of Balkrishna Doshi in Aranya township, Indore, India. His solution to the problem of housing the poor and improving social harmony at a time of social strife is a landmark project. The Kampung Kali Cho-de in Yogyakarta is an important example of what can be achieved when liberal-minded professionals assist social 'outcasts' to transform not only their living conditions but also their sense of community. While the Fortaleza programme in Brazil has been so successful that it has influenced government policy and received an award for excellence in improving the living environment at the Habitat II conference.

ARANYA LOW-COST HOUSING *INDORE, INDIA*

Lailun Ekram

Public authorities seeking to involve local communities have adopted two approaches to housing. First, improving and upgrading the existing slums and, second, providing serviced sites for new housing developments to be built by the people themselves. Aranya Nagar, a township of 88.6 hectares, was a site-and-services project with core units for a new housing development of some 6,500 dwellings. The Indore Development Authority (IDA) aimed to meet the needs of sixty thousand people, most of whom were poor (a group referred to as the Economically Weaker Sector (EWS).

Existing slum settlements in Indore provided an interesting insight into how the poor build for themselves when faced by severe constraints on land and resources. One of the basic characteristics of these communities is multiple and mixed land use. While unplanned and crowded, they nonetheless exhibit certain characteristics and a language of settlement. Huts are built in clusters and form small neighbourhoods. Individual homes extend into the outdoors – what Charles Correa has called the open-to-sky space. Small shops operate within the congested areas, and whenever possible, a tree is planted to create a small public space. In these settlements, streets are not just corridors for movement, they also accommodate various social, economic and domestic activities and, in doing so, enhance the quality of the living environment. The presence of the small shops highlights their relevance in the neighbourhood as a means of earning a livelihood with minimum investment.

The Aranya site is approximately 1 kilometre square, and is approached by the Bombay–Delhi national highway on its eastern side. Along this boundary, 1.85 hectares has been set aside to accommodate the existing light industries. General and service industries are within 1.5 to 2 kilometres on the western and northern sides respectively. All these non-residential activities create ample job opportunities for the people living in the surrounding areas.

In 1983, the Vastu-Shilpa Foundation for Studies and Research in Environmental Design was entrusted with the task of preparing a master plan with innovative options to develop a township in Aranya (Aranya means forest). Its general objectives were:

— to create a new township that has a sense of continuity with existing settlement patterns,

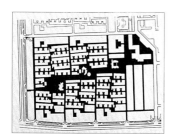

Detail of one sector of the master plan showing overlapping community spaces

Demonstration housing designed by the architect Balkrishna Doshi

Over time the residents decorate and alter the demonstration houses

The demonstration houses that were built as the first phase of the project

Streets provide outdoor spaces for various activities, such as street trading

Streets and public areas in each cluster provide places for social gathering

retaining the fundamental values of security, and to plan a good living environment;
— to achieve a settlement/township character by harmoniously integrating people and their built environment;
— to create a balanced community of the various socio-economic groups, encouraging co-operation, fraternity, tolerance and self-help generated through a physical planning process;
— to evolve a framework where incremental development can take place within a legal, economical and organisational framework.
The design was approached at different levels which eventually resulted in the creation of neighbourhoods, living areas, working areas, thoroughfares, landscaping and public spaces.

At the township level, the aim was to provide a central spine for the sectors through the creation of a Central Business District. On one hand this acts as a focus for the sectors, and on the other it reaches out through them – open spaces and public pathways linking the central spine and housing clusters.

The master plan of the township was informal, imitating that of existing slum settlements. It emphasised hierarchical spaces, a central location for basic community services, and allowance for future densification in the context of the Indian lifestyle. It also segregated pedestrian and vehicular movement, and ensured good distribution of built and open space to optimise land use and infrastructure. A further aim was to reflect local characteristics in built-form.

At the community/street level, the aim was to produce a design that integrated the human and built-form scales through the creation of streets based on plugged cluster houses. Not only are these aesthetically pleasing, their design also encourages community interaction: on the *otta* (outdoor platform), an important feature of the Indian home, in the service spaces between houses, and the community spaces and the cul-de-sacs. Spaces at the street corners are varied with an alternating arrangement of road, green space, and pedestrian pathway.

At the dwelling level, a service core was provided. Optional plans answered the prime objective of being sensitive to the lifestyle and daily needs of the inhabitants, and freely inte-

grated indoor and outdoor spaces. Priority was given to orientation, light, ventilation and climatic control; to future scope for vertical expansion and the provision of subletting and commercial options; and to the use of appropriate utility technology, materials and construction methods.

The master plan was divided into six sectors organised around the central spine of commercial and institutional land use. The town centre in the middle part of the spine consists of four clusters of shopping, residential and office complexes. Two more clusters of social functions were located at the end of the spine. This is a mixed-use zone with a five-storey building.

While Aranya was primarily designed for the Economically Weaker Sector, all sections of society are catered for in order to ensure a balanced development. The High Income Group (9 per cent of the community) is distributed along the periphery of the national highway and part of the south-east border of the arterial road in the south. The Middle Income Group (14 per cent of the community) is planned along the periphery of arterial roads on the north-west sides and part on the south arterial road along that part of spine. The Lower Income Group (11 per cent of the community) and the Economically Weaker Sector (65 per cent of the community) are located in the middle of all six sectors.

The options of core housing for the EWS included:
— site, plinth and service-core (latrine and water tap);
— site, plinth and service-core (latrine and bath);
— site, plinth and service-core (latrine and bath) and one room (kitchen).
For other income groups only plots were sold. A verandah or house extension helped in expanding the small EWS houses and enhanced the quality of space. A transition zone of 0.5 metres between the street and house was provided. Permissible house extensions such as platforms, porches, balconies and open stairs were built, and contributed to a varied street character.

Each house plan included two rooms and a living area followed by a kitchen and a lavatory set between the front extension and the multi-use courtyard at the back. Most houses are also provided with additional access at the back, allowing animals – or a vehicle – to be kept, or even for part of the house to be rented out to provide income.

Ten houses form a cluster that opens into the street. The courtyards at the back of the houses open onto the open space of the cluster which can be used as a play and service area; trees and a multi-use platform were added.

These open areas link up to the central spine and form a triangular space incorporating a community function. A staggered flow of space, this path forms an intimate system of niches and corners for the community. A pedestrian pathway intersects this green strip with three connecting squares ending in the third cul-de-sac square. A secondary stepped pathway with a consecutive overlapping square flows into the housing blocks at right angles to the 4.5-metre street. These spaces open to the street and allow the families to intact as one community.

The most important aspect of this project was the process of implementation and the manner in which design was used to help build social cohesion across sectarian lines.

The Vastu-Shilpa Foundation carried out considerable research into the Aranya housing scheme. Detailed surveys were conducted to understand the physical and economic factors that determine the size, type and density of plots. Planners and architects designed the total scheme from the financial planning to the structural stage. They produced a kit of components with detailed drawings from which home owners could then construct their houses.

A section of the master plan was constructed to create a demonstration model of housing showing alternative layouts. In this way Aranya's residents were familiarised with the building systems, techniques, structures and materials. Model houses included one-, two- and three-storey houses in brick.

The funding agencies were the Housing and Urban Development Co-operative (HUDCO) and the World Bank. To ensure that the scheme could be replicated, the World Bank insisted that a minimum of 65 per cent of plots be affordable by the EWS without any external subsidies. However, some cross-subsidisation within the project was accepted, based on profits generated by selling plots at the market rate to members of the Higher Income Group. Commercial plots were auctioned. The project was a financial as well as a design success.

The cost recovered was Rs614.28 whereas the development cost was Rs548.47, a surplus generated due to accrued interest. There was a surplus in the project cost. The interest rate was 12 per cent on a twenty-year loan.

The gross cost per square metre was Rs71.23 for the total development. The average monthly income of the EWS was Rs700. Depending on the plot size, the down payment for allotment of the plot was fixed at Rs200, Rs300 and Rs400;

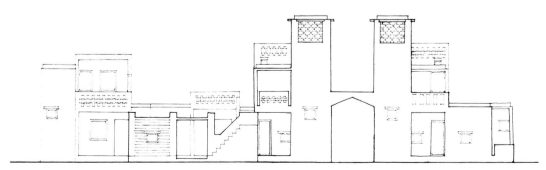

Elevations of demonstration houses

the loan balance was Rs2,103, Rs3,593, and Rs7,748; the monthly instalment was Rs23.23, Rs39.52 and Rs85.23 respectively. Thus credit was central to the success of the programme.

A monthly maintenance charge was fixed at Rs2 for all EWS plots. During the early days of the project, plots were allotted on a first-come basis. As the project gained momentum, there was a high number of applicants and the plots had to be awarded based on a lottery.

The installation of utilities and infrastructure took place incrementally as the residents paid their monthly instalment. The community decided on the priority of services on a consensus basis.

In assessing the success of the scheme, it is clear that the role of the professional played a central role. This ranged from designing the overall layout, which is so different from the standard grids that plague so many site-and-services schemes, to developing the elegant and flexible architectural vocabulary of the model homes. The integration of the well defined hierarchy of built form and open space was responsive to the needs and aspirations of the people. But perhaps more important were the architect's efforts to use the design process to help build a sense of community between the different cultural, ethnic and religious groups. A sense of community is encouraged by the informality of the master plan, the house plan and land use; by the need for neighbours to co-operate in the building of shared facilities; and by the presence of the shared *otta* between them.

This was important because the distribution of the groups corresponds to their general incidence in the greater population. Eighty per cent of the inhabitants of Aranya are Hindu, 12.7 per cent are Muslim, with the rest a mixture of Buddhist, Christian, Sikh, Jains and others. Many have different linguistic backgrounds, including Gujarati, Hindi and Urdu. Enforcing this social cohesion, residents are aware of the importance of action groups and community groups to make decisions and manage the living environment.

All in all, this is a remarkable success. It shows the involvement of the professional architects and planners at their best, while reflecting the logic of the architecture of empowerment, giving the poor the opportunity to shape their own destinies. Crucially, it has also been successful in engaging the residents in becoming good neighbours rather than sullen or hostile co-existing groups, as is frequently the case in other parts of India. Underlying the design is the concept of tolerance, of people learning to live next to each other and learning to live by consensus, sharing values within physical, cultural and contextural parameters. Architecture has thus been able to celebrate the life of common people – the prime objective of the Aranya township design.

The project has become a research and training institution for students of sociology, planning and architecture; technocrats in government departments; professionals and practitioners; and donor agencies and their representatives. It was awarded the Aga Khan award for Architecture in 1995.

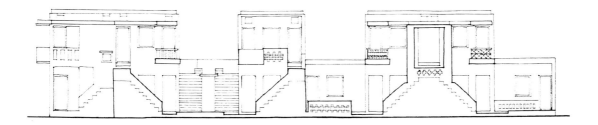

KAMPUNG KALI CHO-DE
YOGYAKARTA, INDONESIA

Ismaïl Serageldin

Kampung Kali Cho-de is a squatter-type village settlement, illegal but tolerated by the government. It is built on a refuse dump on the banks of the River Cho-de in Yogyakarta, central Java. Prior to 1983, the village of around thirty-five families was a poor, unhealthy slum. In 1983, YB Mangunwijaya, an architect and social worker with previous experience of kampung improvement, and Willi Prasetya, the village leader, succeeded in establishing a permanent co-operative system, which was accepted and acknowledged by the government. Previous plans to demolish the settlement in order to promote a clean, green river bank were laid aside. Volunteer, unskilled labour was provided by the villagers; technical skills and fund management by YB Mangunwijaya, and political liaison by Willi Prasetya.

The kampung is openly situated on a long, narrow, very steep strip of land under the Gondolayu Bridge, a prominent circulation route in Yogyakarta. The settlement is on the east bank of the river, hemmed in by existing garages. This very constrained site was one of the main challenges which the project had to overcome.

The process of empowerment started by building Balairukum Tetangga, 'House of the Brotherhood of Neighbours', to allow the neces-sary process of dialogue and consensus to determine priorities within the village. This was followed by the reinforcement of retaining walls on a site subject to occasional flooding, and the construction of several model houses. Subsequently, homes were replaced as required by an urban version of the traditional tribal house, each room requiring Rp50 per day contribution to the co-operative. Later, structures were added to house homeless children, guests and visitors. The structures themselves are lightweight, due to extremely poor soil conditions, and are raised above the ground on pilotis; the construction materials – bamboo and coconut wood – are readily available which also facilitates future maintenance. The installation of electricity by the government is seen as an official acceptance of the settlement which continues to be developed, administered and maintained by the kampung inhabitants.

Though the construction of the buildings is very modest, the improvements are striking. The main frame is timber with bamboo secondary support resting on local stone point foundations, with coconut wood and bamboo infill panels. Floors are plaited bamboo mats. Roofs are covered in terracotta tiling or corrugated iron sheet.

Wedged within a tiny enclave, the kampung developed its distinctive identity

Water is supplied from the river

The tiny spaces between the buildings are also used for social gatherings

The real significance of the project, however, is that through their own efforts, the residents have attained self-respect and the respect of the community. The success of the improvements extended to assisting local homeless people, and seems to have resulted in a rethinking of local government approaches to similar situations. Further, the project's momentum has continued with the planting of gardens and good maintenance. The use of local, native materials has stimulated interest in such an approach from architecture students. The excellence of the project was recognised by an Aga Khan Award for Architecture in 1989.

(Based on information provided by the Aga Khan Award for Architecture's library and documentation services.)

The main frame structures are decorated and are an expression of community identity and self-respect

COMMUNITY-BASED URBANISATION AND FAVELAS REHABILITATION PROCESSES, *FORTALEZA, BRAZIL*

Mona Serageldin, Boguslaw Trondowski and Sameh Wahba
in co-operation with Patrick Bodart and Yves Cabannes

. . . Needy families have a chance to improve their day to day life, and even their relationships.
(Comunidades Association member)

Fortaleza's interlinked urban programmes (Mutirão 50, Comunidades, Casa Melhor and the Integration Council) created a framework for co-ordinated public and community action to address the human aspects as well as the environmental dimensions of rapid urbanisation. The programmes combined capacity building, participation, civic engagement and community-based management of local resources.

Fortaleza, the capital of the Ceará state, in the northern region of Brazil, has a population of 2.5 million inhabitants, over half of whom live in more than 350 irregular settlements known as *favelas*, which lack infrastructure and services. Rapid demographic growth and sustained migration from rural areas has fuelled their proliferation. Since 1973, a new *favela* has developed every month.

In the early seventies, the Municipality of Fortaleza launched a 'defavelisation' programme in parallel with a State Government effort to build large housing estates. The programme's inability to keep up with population growth led to a search for alternative approaches. In 1987, the State and the Municipality initiated a housing programme for low-income families relying on the traditional self-help system known as *mutirões*. To date, more than eleven thousand units have been built by their future occupants. In addition, a social assistance programme PROAFA has also been a dynamic factor in engaging *favelas* communities in the development effort. Finally, in 1988, these projects led the Municipality of Fortaleza, the popular council of Rondon district, and GRET (a French NGO with funding from the French government and the European Community) to sign a partnership agreement to set up a programme for the development of a micro-settlement, Mutirão 50, in one of the poorest districts of Fortaleza.

The success of this pilot project housing fifty low-income families, led the State Government to back the expansion of this community-based initiative. The resulting statewide Comunidades

Women in the communal workshop produce prefabricated blocks by assembling bricks

A construction crew can assemble a dwelling unit every day using the prefabricated blocks

Workers trained by association are operating a carpentry micro-enterprise

programme focuses on fringe areas located beyond the city's administrative boundaries. Projects are sited strategically, generally adjacent to very poor, under-serviced informal settlements. They bring badly needed services to the urban periphery and create vigorous nodes around which sound urban expansion can occur.

The goal of the Mutirão 50 pilot and the Comunidades programmes was to create an interface for co-ordinated action by the different groups involved in urban development. The process capitalises on the complementary roles of NGOs that have the capacity to innovate and lead an outreach and mobilisation effort, and the public authorities that can foster institutionalisation and replication of successful actions. The programmes have three strategic objectives: to create a setting for self-built *mutirões* housing; to generate employment opportunities; and to set in motion a process of sustainable development.

The programmes reinforce citizen participation and the autonomy of community-based organisations by building up their capacity to negotiate with public authorities and broadening their vision and understanding of the wider socio-economic context. The Comunidades programme is managed by a special commission, referred to as the Integration Council. This includes two representatives of each of the partners involved: the State, the municipalities, the university and the technical school, the NGOs and the community groups. The council prepares the annual work plan; co-ordinates public, private and community inputs; ensures the integrated implementation of the different programme components; and discusses with the community the allocation of financial assistance to the programme activities. Separate agreements are signed by the different partners involved in each project, defining the roles, responsibilities and financial commitments of each of the partners.

Close ties to education and research institutions help develop innovative approaches to the three complementary and integrated action lines of the programme: housing construction, institutional development, and job creation. In light of the importance given to technical training, the collaborative effort with educational institutions

is considered critical to the programme's success.

The programmes are committed to the introduction and dissemination of building technology, previously tested in other contexts, that is labour intensive and efficient, providing good quality construction at a reduced cost. For example, the use of pre-assembled reinforced hollow brick blocks, a system successfully used in Argentina, proved very efficient in the Brazilian context when it was first tested in Pacatuba in 1995. Workers with no previous training are able to produce on site the first assembled blocks in less than two weeks. The process has opened up employment opportunities for women engaged in the assembly of blocks.

The project areas are micro-settlements covering from one to three hectares and comprising fifty houses per hectare. It is planned to integrate them into the city's fabric as the urban agglomeration expands. Because of the range of services they offer, including shops and workshops, community facilities and public spaces, they act as structuring elements shaping the city's growth. The sites have full infrastructure services, including a water purification station, as well as adequate landscaping. The market area forms an active centre for social life, grouping a number of small shops, community facilities including a nursery, the Association headquarters and housing for the elderly.

Community associations are organised in each project area and a community fund managed by the Association is established. The fund derives resources from members' contributions and rents from workshops and commercial premises. Title to the land is initially transferred by the Municipality to the community. Later, the Association grants usufruct rights to members with good standing records of no less than five years.

To foster action at a scale commensurate with the dimensions of Brazil's demographic and economic challenges, the Comunidades programme must be replicated throughout the region. With the State acting as catalyst and facilitator for a decentralised local action programme, municipalities and communities can mobilise and pool resources to improve the efficiency and sustainability of development processes based on self-reliance. In the Comunidades, municipalities receive technical and financial assistance from the State to discharge their responsibilities in this joint endeavour. Their role includes land acquisition, implementation of infrastructure works, and training of municipal staff engaged in the interface with communities.

Unlike the conventional *mutirões* which function through specially created management groups, the Mutirão 50 project and the Comunidades programme work through existing community groups. However, new associations are organised as needed to operate specific programme components and to manage the built environment. Special funds are established to finance these independently operated subsidiaries and spin-offs.

The job creation component is a cornerstone of the Mutirão 50 and Comunidades concepts. The central element in each project is the workshop which is the first component built on the site. The workshop produces building materials, prefabricated components, and pre-assembled elements for housing construction. The energies of future residents are marshalled through a structured system designed to simultaneously ensure their participation in the community building process, to increase the efficiency of self-built construction, and to improve the skills in the building trades. This main workshop, serving principally the *mutirões*, anchors an economic activity zone where interlinked or independent micro-enterprises can be started by residents living in both the project areas and the surrounding settlements.

The State government has established a credit line to encourage start-up businesses in the industrial zone. Entrepreneurs can obtain seed capital to purchase equipment and working capital for their operations. Loans are reimbursable over a one-year period. The fund is replenished through borrowers' savings and loan repayments, allocations from community association funds, and contributions from the municipalities concerned.

In parallel, a credit mechanism has been established to finance the rehabilitation of *favelas* within the municipal boundaries of Fortaleza. The Casa Melhor credit programme offers loans at zero interest, reimbursable over a one year period, to families and individuals who have legal ownership or occupancy rights to the housing they reside in, for the purpose of rehabilitating and improving their dwellings. The Community Association reviews and guarantees the applicants and participates with GRET and the Mayor's office in the programme's administration. Implementation of the process is ensured by Cereah Periferia, a local NGO. Residents may apply for a maximum of three loans for the same property. Loan amounts consist of varying proportions of borrowers' savings, municipal subsidy, and GRET credit. The municipal subsidy, initially equivalent to 30 per cent, is decreased to 15 per cent for the second loan and is completely phased out in the third loan. The declining subsidy is offset by increasing contributions from borrowers' savings. By 1996, more than one thousand applicants in forty-one suburbs contracted loans.

The Mutirão 50 project and the Comunidades programme differ from conventional sites-and-services projects in their concept, design and implementation.

— Locations of project areas are selected to maximise spillover effects and shape urban growth.
— Resident participation is an integral component of every programme activity and is structured to foster inclusion, capacity building and self-reliance.
— Job creation is a key strategic objective focusing on opening employment opportunities for residents in the project areas and adjacent settlements.
— Implementation relies on empowerment transforming beneficiaries into stake holders through community control of development and management processes.

Fortaleza's interlinked urban programmes were selected from six hundred submissions as one of twelve Best Practices to receive an award for excellence in improving the living environment at the Habitat II conference, in June 1996.

'. . . the programme strengthened our entity.'
(Comunidades Association member)

MANAGING THE URBAN ENVIRONMENT

The highest cost of urban environmental problems is borne by human health, and most of all by that of the poor. Yet the main environmental problems affecting human health – lead, dust, soot and microbial disease – can all be solved with only modest expenditure. Action should be taken now. Lead in petrol should be phased out at an accelerated rate. Basic services, primarily clean water and sanitation, should be provided for all city dwellers. This measure is affordable. Many investments to reduce emissions of dust, soot and smoke from industry and power plants have high returns. They should be made. So why aren't they? The answer lies partly in the citizens not being sufficiently involved. The case of Curitiba, Brazil, is both dramatic and instructive.

URBAN MANAGEMENT AND THE ENVIRONMENT
CURITIBA, BRAZIL

Michael Cohen

Curitiba has been widely hailed for its enlightened urban transport network, its energy management, and its attention to environmental protection. While much attention and credit has been given to its former dynamic mayor, Jaime Lerner, now Governor of Paraná State, the institutional foundations for Curitiba's exemplary performance lie in two generations of planners and policy-makers who considered alternative development paths for the city. As a rapidly growing area in the early 1970s, Curitiba faced the common problems of a rapidly expanding metropolitan area. In contrast to many other cities, the planners of the early 1970s decided to pursue a long-term vision of sustainable development rather than merely to develop a series of individual projects. Over time, this has produced dramatic results.

Public transport was the first sector addressed. A unified approach was developed with large city buses on main routes connecting to smaller buses and neighbourhood vehicles. This transport hierarchy was supported by efficiently designed transfer stations and reliable service. By 1992, efficient public and private urban transport had led to a reduction in private car usage of 35 per cent in a city of two million – unheard of in any city in the world, with the exception of Havana. This drop in single-car trips resulted in both energy savings and reduced air pollution. The use of the bus tubes, stations where passengers paid their fares before getting on the buses, further reduced stopping times and increased overall speed of service. This led then-Mayor Lerner to refer to the system as an 'above ground subway'.

The second critical sector for innovation was solid waste management. Curitiba is the only city in the world which rewards its citizens who recycle their waste with free vegetables or those who bring their rubbish to central locations with bus tokens. These popular programmes have helped to mobilise community awareness of the importance of recycling and environmental sanitation at the neighbourhood level. City garbage trucks carry signs about using 'garbage which is not garbage'. In many cases, the recycling process has led to new jobs, for example, in making toys from objects which have been discarded. Mayor Lerner invited some of Brazil's leading designers to visit Curitiba in the early 1990s to see how they could use these objects to make toys and other items.

While these innovative techniques have produced outstanding improvements in environmental sanitation, they have been reinforced by a broader city-wide commitment to public health. Curitiba has established more than one hundred public daycare centres where low-income children receive three balanced meals each day and health care. The city boasts lower levels of malnutrition than other Brazilian cities of comparable size. Moreover, citizens are encouraged to exercise. Curitiba has become a city of bicycle riders and joggers in well-maintained public parks.

Yet, beyond these innovations, there is a stronger, more important process of empowerment which gives individuals and communities confidence in their ability to manage the city. Thus, over a thirty-year period, there has been a continuing stream of innovations from an empowered and engaged population. A major component of this process has been public investment in environmental education, starting with public schools. The establishment of an 'Open University for the Environment' in 1990 has resulted in a widely informed population, from all income levels and social origins. Special efforts were made by the Municipality to reach out to particular occupational groups: taxi drivers participated in environmental education classes; insurance agents were educated on how environmental conditions affect health and the prospects of potential clients; and industrial enterprises are carefully monitored and supported in their efforts to choose environmentally friendly technologies and practice.

Reserved bus lanes

Cylindrical bus stops

Taken together, all of these efforts have led to a shared sense of civic and environmental responsibility in the city. Perhaps the best testimonial to this process has been the fact that it has not stopped with the departure of Mayor Lerner, but has been enthusiastically extended by the new mayor.

MICRO-FINANCE: REACHING THE POOREST
Ismaïl Serageldin

Over one billion people continue to live in abject poverty; some 70 per cent of them are women. Every day forty thousand people die of hunger-related causes. They are the ones who benefit last and benefit least from the process of economic development. For them to acquire a minimum level of food, shelter and decent living requires that they be empowered to improve their economic opportunities. Micro-finance appears the most promising way to reach them.

While ample evidence exists to show that broad-based, sustainable economic growth coupled with improved access to education, health care and social services reduces poverty, the poorest need a special outreach effort. In other words, measures to reduce poverty and hunger work well when sound macro-economic policy is matched with effective micro-level interventions.

The preceding case studies in this book demonstrate how architects and planners have acted to empower the weak and the marginalised in successful outreach projects, often with spectacular results in terms of improvements in well-being and the built environment. Throughout these programmes, access to credit is a recurring theme. The questions of how best to provide access to credit for the very poor is the subject of this section. This is the financial equivalent of the architecture of empowerment.

Why Micro-Finance?
Providing financial services such as credit and savings to the poor has proved effective in raising their employment, income and living standards. Higher income for the poor results in increased investments in education, nutrition and household welfare leading to an improvement in the quality of life. In developing countries the micro-enterprise sector employs an estimated 30 to 80 per cent of the economically active population.

This people-centred approach to micro-finance was pioneered by specialised NGOs and commercial banks such as the Grameen Bank (Bangladesh), BRI-Unit Desa (Indonesia), K-Rep (Kenya), and Prodem/BancoSol (Bolivia) among others. They have demonstrated that the poor are in fact creditworthy, that they can be given credit without collateral, that they are not asking for handouts or subsidies, but only the opportunity to improve their lot. The results have been spectacular, especially when the credit is supported by some essential non-financial services as well.

These pioneers have shown that populations traditionally excluded by the formal financial sector can, in fact, be a market niche for innovative banking services that are commercially sustainable. Micro-finance represents a significant departure from earlier exercises in providing credit to the poor through financial institutions at subsidised rates with little or no recovery rate. Successful micro-finance institutions are (largely) local organisations that reach a neglected sector and are commercially viable, or well on the way to be so.

How Significant is the Sector?
Contrary to what some may think, the micro-finance sector is significant, and growing fast. A 1996 world-wide inventory of micro-finance institutions found that they numbered over a thousand (that is, institutions that had been in operation for three years and reached at least one thousand borrowers). Although a handful of giants with more than one million borrowers each (the Grameen Bank and BRI-UD, for example) dominated the picture, there were also at least six thousand smaller institutions not covered by the survey. The big difficulty appears to be in scaling up, in capacity building at grass roots.

The figures, however, are still stunning: by September 1995, these one thousand institutions had $7 billion amazing in thirteen million loans. In 1994 alone they issued thirty-three million loans to their clients. Even more important, the growth rate was an amazing 31 per cent between 1993 and 1994 – also a risk factor if they are to maintain their outstanding repayment rates which usually stand at near 97 per cent. The vast majority of the successful credit programmes reach out to women. On the savings side, they have reached forty-five million poor people and mobilised $19 billion in deposits.

Making Micro-Finance More Effective

However, despite these successes, two areas still need to be addressed. First, these programmes need to expand their coverage – fewer than 2 per cent of low-income entrepreneurs have access to financial services. Second, the key to their effectiveness lies in sustainability: they must be able to function without continuous subsidies. Only thus will micro-finance come into its own and be self-replicating on a scale that will have a real impact on global poverty. A report by Women's World Banking has identified several recommendations for the sustainable provision of savings and credit services to the poor.

Access and Standards: All major players need to agree that the issue is to provide access, not subsidies, to low-income entrepreneurs. Efficient financial intermediaries need to charge high enough rates to cover the costs of making small loans, so that they can replicate their programmes and reach large numbers of the poor.

Those institutions that meet high standards of financial performance, client reach and business practices, or are credibly on their way to meeting them, should have access to capitalisation, loan funds, and effective capacity building support. This last is critical to help organisations at different stages of development move to sustainable scales of operation. Support should be structured as a catalyst and complement to savings and other domestic resource mobilisation measures by the local level (or retail) institutions that are interfacing with the clients. Legal frameworks, second-tier institutions and effective financing arrangements are needed.

Build Dynamic Performance Standards: Performance standards are essential, but they must

be designed to match the level of development of the service-providing institution. Thus both incremental and absolute standards need to be established on financial performance, client reach and business practices. It is important that all involved parties – be they funders, second-tier institutions, retail intermediaries or regulatory bodies – understand, endorse and adopt the same principles, objectives and bases for determining performance. There should be different thresholds for accessing different types and levels of support.

Support Institutions Not Projects: Before financial intermediaries reach the size where they can be fully self-sustaining they will need help; early operations will need to be subsidised. NGOs and other specialised financial intermediaries, which are not in the position to cross-subsidise micro-enterprise lending while they build lending volumes, will need some form of institutional subsidy for a period of five to seven years. Specialised institutions that meet performance standards need capitalisation and low-cost, long-term loan funds, preferably repayable in local currency, while they expand their volumes to sustainable levels. As institutions expand their micro-financing operations, they will need access to effective capacity-building services. The main means will be practitioner training, institution-specific technical services, and benchmarking against best practice. The most effective sources of institutional development support tend to be practitioner networks, not foreign academic or institutional consultants.

Emphasise Savings and Domestic Resource Mobilisation: Savings services can be as important as loan services to micro-enterprises. Deposit mobilisation can also be one of the most effective means for intermediaries to mobilise resources. Savings mobilisation makes financial institutions accountable to local shareholders. All financial intermediaries that lend to micro-enterprises should be encouraged to build savings mobilisation arrangements for their clients, either by providing these services directly, or by making arrangements with another financial institution. Banking regulations need to be adapted to encourage those micro-financing institutions with the capabilities to legally mobilise savings from clients or the general public.

Match Services to Clients' Needs: Client-friendly services are the key to doing business with the very poor, who are understandably wary of formal institutions and will not necessarily approach them of their own accord. The micro-financier must be governed by an outreach mentality and an empathy for the clients, and should avoid a one-product fits all outlook.

Provide Financing that Fits the Institution: If governments and external funders are to help build financial institutions that serve the majority, namely the poor, they will need to adopt new funding approaches. These include:
— small amounts of grant funds for promising new entrants to finance start-up operating costs and loan portfolios over a short period;
— capitalisation for institutions that meet performance standards;
— access to refinance from development banks and other second-tier intermediaries;
— partial loan guarantees to encourage the build-up of leveraged credit lines by local banks to specialised financial intermediaries.

Once an institution is large and efficient enough to cover costs and manage fully commercial sources, it will be able to access international commercial funds directly and through networks.

Utilise Second-Tier Institutions: A second-tier institution is a financial intermediary or network that provides financial and institutional support services to retail intermediaries. Development banks and practitioner networks have major roles to play over the next five to ten years, as wholesalers of capitalisation, refinance and institutional development support, in:
— building an agreed set of standards as the eligibility criteria for accessing support services;
— organising performance benchmarking systems;

— encouraging exchange of experience among participating retail institutions;
— serving as a wholesaler or broker of seed funding, capitalisation funds, refinance of loan funds, and institutional development support;
— encouraging mutually advantageous linkages between commercial banks and specialised financial intermediaries;
— helping ensure that the appropriate legal, regulatory and supervisory structures and incentives are in place.

To succeed in providing these services, the second-tier institution needs to be autonomous, and free from political interference; have the capabilities to mobilise funding; know the retail institutions intimately; and be able to motivate retail institutions while being tough in the enforcement of standards and eligibility criteria for support.

Build the Regulatory and Incentive Framework: Governments are key to establishing an enabling environment for micro-financing institutions. In building policies, regulations and incentives for financial institutions that serve the poor, several principles and practices are crucial:
— a range of institutions should be encouraged to enter and expand;
— micro-financing institutions that meet performance standards should be allowed to operate as recognised financial intermediaries;
— entry thresholds, such as minimum capital requirements, should be kept low enough to allow specialised institutions to become part of the formal financial system;
— supervisory and reporting requirements should be kept simple, with a focus on key performance indicators;
— institutions lending to micro- and small enterprises should be free to set their on-lending interest rates;
— attractive incentives should be provided to these intermediaries.

The Consultative Group to Assist the Poorest

A recent innovation in this field of micro-finance is the Consultative Group to Assist the Poorest (CGAP), established with the aim of broadening

Recipients of the successful micro-finance programme of the Grameen Bank, Bangladesh

and deepening the success of micro-finance. The objectives of CGAP are to: (i) support micro-finance institutions that deliver credit and/or savings services to the very poor on a financially sustainable basis; (ii) increase learning and dissemination of best practice for delivering financial services to the poor; (iii) strengthen donor co-ordination in the field of micro-finance; (iv) create an enabling environment for micro-lending institutions; (v) help improve access of low-income groups to financial services by identifying institutional and policy deficiencies; (vi) help establish providers of micro-finance to assist others start such services.

CGAP was formally constituted on 27 June 1995 with the participation of nine member donors (now twenty-three), who jointly pledged roughly US$300 million to the CGAP portfolio. The majority of that funding is being administered directly by the participating member donors. The World Bank's cash contribution of US$30 million is the basis of a three-year 'core-fund' that is administered by the CGAP Secretariat to support eligible micro-finance institutions. The members of CGAP hope to:

— develop criteria, operating procedures, and guidelines by which proposals from micro-finance institutions will be appraised and evaluated;
— distil and disseminate lessons on operational and policy issues;
— co-ordinate donor activity in micro-finance to improve effectiveness of support to deserving enterprises and reduce bureaucracy and paperwork.

The CGAP relies on a Policy Advisory Group (PAG) to support and advise the Consultative Group and the Secretariat on policy and operational issues – on the overall direction of CGAP; and to assure that the best practical knowledge is available. This Advisory Group comprises eleven distinguished experts in the field of micro-finance, chaired by Muhammad Yunus of the Grameen Bank.

One of the key goals of the CGAP is to mainstream micro-finance within the regular operations of the World Bank and other financiers. This would remove the financial constraint on the effective support of worthy micro-finance ventures. Within that framework, the World Bank can play a pivotal role in working with governments to create an enabling business environment for micro-finance institutions, and making linkages between the overall macro-economic framework and micro-finance.

This type of mainstreaming is important. For example, the World Bank can provide assistance in improving the legal and regulatory environment for micro-enterprises, and in carrying out financial sector reforms that are conducive to sustainable micro-finance institutions. Such reforms include: removal of ceilings on interest rates and competing subsidised credit schemes, less restrictive banking laws, and prudential regulation and supervision to accommodate non-bank financial institutions (particularly those involved in savings mobilisation and uncollateralised credit to individuals through solidarity groups), and changing property rights/collateral laws. The CGAP Secretariat will promote learning among

World Bank staff on how to integrate micro-finance issues into lending operations and apply best practice lessons.

The CGAP will also fund eligible micro-finance institutions. A variety of financial institutions such as NGOs, credit unions, co-operatives, and banks that meet the established criteria are eligible for financing, and some have started receiving such funds. Funds from the ($30 million) grant facility are meant to leverage other available donor/private sector resources to increase the capabilities and reach of micro-finance institutions. CGAP focuses on programmes that are reaching out to poor women.

CGAP as a Learning by Doing Forum

This initiative represents perhaps the greatest challenge for the donor community. For the first time, donors will join forces to collaboratively expand the level of resources available to the very poor, especially poor women, and deepen the reach in order to serve those who are in the greatest need.

The CGAP framework will allow practitioners to learn from each other. It will allow donors to learn how best to support the expansion of successful programmes so that they reach greater numbers of those in need as well as the poorer segment of the population. It will allow governments to learn how they can better create a climate in which such successful micro-lending institutions can flourish. In addition, it will allow donors, such as the World Bank, to incorporate the lessons learned into its regular operations thus creating an important multiplier effect for the CGAP's own efforts. The Policy Advisory Group of CGAP is an essential vehicle to bring practitioners into the decision-making of CGAP and thus make it a more effective instrument for forging real partnerships with those who are working with the poor on a daily basis.

Beyond CGAP: The Micro-Finance Summit

Eradicating hunger and poverty is an attainable goal, but it can only be achieved by co-ordinated efforts at the international level and by ensuring the participation of the poor in improving their own living conditions. The latter can be best achieved by providing the poor with the tools they need to help themselves: micro-finance is one such proven tool. To make this effective, there must be partnerships and continuous and systematic dialogue between micro-finance practitioners, NGOs, the private sector, governments – both national and local – and international agencies. The Micro-Finance Summit held in Washington, DC, in February 1997 has been convened to give this process focus and power. Its explicit goal is to engage all parties to work towards reaching one hundred million new borrowers among the poor by 2005 (assuming that a family unit consists of five members, the summit thus aims to benefit five hundred million).

The effort is being spearheaded by Sam Daley-Harris of the Results Educational Fund, an umbrella organisation which brings together 1,700 NGOs under the aegis of Results International. It is noteworthy that the summit has received enthusiastic support from heads of state and governments, as well as those of international agencies and private banks. Gifted micro-finance and development practitioners are serving on the organising committee, which augurs well for the success of the summit and its ten-year plan.

Micro-financiers, the architects of empowerment in the broadest sense, have already implemented successful schemes that have enabled the poor to attain decent living standards. It is up to us to ensure that the best practices of some become the standard practices of all, and that the future is brighter for that large part of humanity that still lacks the means to meet its basic needs.

(Based on information prepared by the World Bank, WWB and CGAP, distilled by Mohini Malhotra and Eveling Bermudez)

EPILOGUE
Muhammad Yunus and Ismaïl Serageldin

The preceding essays and case studies all share some essential features. They put people at the centre of the development process. They rely on the innate abilities of the poor to solve their own problems, with the technicians – be they architects or financiers – largely in a supporting role. The poor are the artisans of their own well-being, they become empowered to take charge of their own destinies: this is the essence of the architecture of empowerment.

It is an architecture which stresses context, without which buildings have no meaning. This context is partly physical – in terms of infrastructure, other buildings and amenities – and partly abstract – in the sense of community and the opportunities to better one's livelihood. The architecture of empowerment is concerned with creating communities and strengthening the social capital that binds them together.

The Grameen Bank's pioneering micro-credit scheme is well known, but equally important is its enlightened social agenda: its focus on solidarity networks to create a basis for mutual support and community bonds, and its emphasis on the broader social issues. These include taking care of the children, eschewing bad practices (such as the ruinous dowries so common among the poorer classes), and generally building self-confidence through the application of the sixteen principles of self-reliance and development.

In the field of micro-finance, the success of the Grameen Bank has demonstrated that the issue is not so much the creditworthiness of the poor, but their access to credit. It has pointed the way to a development process based on empowerment of the weak and the marginalised. The lesson is the same in many of the micro-finance enterprises in the developing countries and even in the industrialised countries of the North. Indeed, here programmes such as Shore Bank in Chicago show that the concept of micro-finance can be transferred successfully from country to country and from society to society because it is not a model applied willy-nilly, but a process that empowers the poor to design their own programmes. It can never be seen as an import, but as the result of local initiative and talent.

Can other professions adopt the same philosophy as the financiers and succeed? The ideas and built schemes presented in this book show that they can. The question is not whether but why: why are the lessons of success not being replicated more systematically everywhere?

We hope that the social activists who support micro-finance will also turn their attention to the built environment. They have accepted the idea of access to credit as a basic human right; access to the resources to build an empowering environment are no less important.

This book shows that the architecture of empowerment is as much about process as it is about product; that it is not limited to the problems of developing countries, but is also relevant to industrialised countries. It is about respecting our common humanity and investing in all the people as the creators of a better future. We must do all that we can to encourage its progress.